FOOD FROM AMERICA'S BRAVEST

R.G. ADAMS

ISLANDOG PUBLICATIONS
ROCHESTER, NEW YORK

FIREHOUSE COOKING: FOOD FROM AMERICA'S BRAVEST

Published by Islandog Publications
423 French Road Rochester NY 14618
www.firehouse-cooking.com

ISBN 0-9638089-1-5

Written, designed and typeset in The United States of America
Printed and bound in Thailand by Sirivatana Interprint PLC

IDP BOOKS ARE AVAILABLE AT QUANTITY DISCOUNTS WHEN USED TO PROMOTE
PRODUCTS, SERVICES, OR CHARITIES RELATING TO THE FIRE SERVICE INDUSTRY.
FOR MORE INFORMATION PLEASE CONTACT OUR SPECIAL MARKETS COORDINATOR.

ISLANDOG PUBLICATIONS
PLEASE CONTACT US AT:
WWW.FIREHOUSE-COOKING.COM

Contents

Dedication

If Prometheus was worthy of the wrath of heaven
for kindling the first fire upon the earth,
how ought all the gods to honor the men
who make it their professional business to put it out?

—John Godfrey Saxe,
American journalist, poet,
and lecturer, ca. 1850

This book is dedicated to our firefighters—some of the most heroic men and women the world has ever known. Everyday they bravely expose themselves to potential peril; often saving us from ourselves and often under-appreciated. This book is a tribute that celebrates both their universal similarities and special uniqueness.

For keeping watch over our lives and property—
I join everyone, everywhere, in saying thank you.

Acknowledgments

I would like to thank the following people who without their input, assistance, and guidance this book would not have been possible. I'm certain it should also be mentioned that their patience has been much appreciated. Over the past ten years as I droned on incessantly about the book and all its many parts, their continuing support never wavered. I am blessed to be surrounded by such supportive people.

Shirley and Mark Adams; Dr. Mark Adams; Dr. Jim Adams; Bill Assimon: Ann and David Beckerman; Donna Benwitz; Bruce Bowling; Maggie Brooks; Rossana Burroni; Peter Durant; Gary Ferrara; John Green; Elaine Hosmer; Micheal Kinnick; Donna Kittrel; Kathy Lindsley; Marcy Lovett; Lisa Lowden; Margery and Eric Fellenzer; Denise McGann; Nick Minieri; Pamela Mostyn; Kate Skestos; Mary Sloan; Cathleen and Douglas Streit; Marilyn Tedeschi; Dr. Bill Valenti; Michael Vinci; Arthur Vitoch; Thomas Warfield and Mark Wert. I'm certain I've missed more than just a few folks, and their omission from this short list does not mean I am not grateful and their contributions diminished.

Photographers & Artists

DENNIS FLOSS
  ROCHESTER, NY: AMERICAN/CANADIAN FLAGS
                  & CHAPTER DIVISION HELMETS
DAVID MAHONEY
  ROCHESTER, NY: COVER PHOTO
CHRIS E. MICKAL
  NEW ORLEANS FIRE DEPARTMENT: PLATE 1 & 2
WILLIAM GREENBLATT
  ST. LOUIS FIRE DEPARTMENT: PLATE 3 & 4
J. L. ALFONSO; GIOVANNI FELIPE; LARRY WEINTRAUB
  MIAMI, FL, FIRE DEPARTMENT: PLATE 5 & 6
SCOTT COWDEN
  TORONTO, ONTARIO, FIRE DEPARTMENT: PLATE 7
RANDY J. KILBURN
  EDMONTON, ALBERTA, FIRE DEPARTMENT: PLATE 8
DAVID J. BLAIRE
  CITY OF LOS ANGELES, CA, FIRE DEPARTMENT: PLATE 9 & 10
CAPTAIN, D.R. (DON) SNIDER; G.M. GHIZ
  HALIFAX, NOVA SCOTIA, FIRE DEPARTMENT: PLATE 11 & 12
DAVID WIIST
  EDMOND, OKLA, FIRE DEPARTMENT: PLATE 13

About the Recipes and Contributors

The recipes in this book were graciously submitted by firefighters from all over the United States and Canada. Nearly ten years ago, I sent out a letter requesting recipes and was overwhelmed by the response. Hundreds of recipes were sent to me over the following few months. I knew then that the men and women in the fire/rescue field were "hungry" for recipes from their fellow firefighters.

I received some duplicate recipes, and others that had appeared in other cookbooks, so not all of them could be used. I apologize to anyone who made a submission and cannot find it in this book. In order to round out the chapters, and to give continuity and variety to the book, I've also included some of my own recipes. They've been collected, over the years, from the many firehouse dinners I've attended.

You'll find that many of these recipes are not the trendy low-fat or low-cholesterol recipes you're likely to find in many other cookbooks. Instead, they reflect the variety and individuality, and the no-nonsense approach of the contributors. I've tried to use simple language and common ingredients, to make this book a resource for the not-so-experienced cook. Most of them are quite simple, but I've snuck in a few slightly more difficult ones for those who are a bit more familiar with the kitchen.

Below I've listed the names of the contributors, with a bit of information about each. Since I've long lost the original source of many of my own contributions, this is by no means a complete list. So a hearty thanks to all who helped. And while my name is on the cover, this is, after all, a cookbook of, by, and for firefighters everywhere.

From the Palm Beach County (Fla.) Fire Department, **Barbara Allred** sent in her unique broccoli salad and spicy chicken casserole recipes.

John Bartchy is a captain with the New Orleans Fire Department and has been with the department for 25 years. His bread pudding with lemon sauce is a must try!

Jerome Bell is a FPS I inspector with the Dayton, Ohio Fire Prevention Bureau. He sends along a combination of standard fire hall favorites with his "Chili Spaghetti" recipe.

Al "Cookieman" Cooke takes his name and his profession seriously. A firefighter with the Edmonton, Alberta, Fire Department, he submitted some of "...his favorites and what seem to be the boys' favorites."

Gerard J. Crowley is a firefighter with the Marine Unit Division, Boston, Massachusetts. He wrote, "As you know, the problem with firehouse cooking is who remembers how much? A pinch of this, a splash of that, a couple of these." I'm glad Gerard took the time to write these down. He included several recipes that are favorites of Group 2.

Bob Dubbert is a 3 year veteran with the Vancouver (B.C.) Fire Department. He is one of 800 firefighters there. His "Chicken Enchilada Casserole" is highly influenced by the diverse culture of Canada's third largest city.

Humble **David Fernandez**, a firefighter with the Tampa Fire Department, provides us with a recipe that bears not only his epicurean taste, but his name as well. "Fettucini Fernandez" is highly recommended.

David R. Harris is a firefighter with the Fulton County (GA) Fire Department in Atlanta, Georgia. He submitted "Rolled Chicken Breast," a favorite at stations #2 and #4.

Debbie Hopkins is a cartographer with the Orange County (Fla.) Fire/ Rescue Communications Center. Debbie is an upstate New York native who has been living in central Florida for 19 years and has been making "Perfect Rice" for 10 of them.

Joe Jolley, a driver with the Tulsa, (Okla.) Fire Department, sends us his "Famous Fabulous Fowl Fajitas From Joe" and "Jolley's Haz-Mat Baked Beans," which is "...guaranteed to produce hazardous gasses."

Darlene Karsevich graciously submitted several recipes. She is a secretary with the City of Winnipeg Fire Department, which has 26 fire departments and a total complement of 979 people bravely serving Winnipeg's population of approximately 930,000 people.

Pat Kunz, working at the Buffalo (N.Y.) Fire Department Bureau of Fire Training, gives us an uptown flavor with her "White Chocolate Chunk and Macadamia Nut Cookies," sure to be the favorite of any cookie lover.

Ted Kurylukis a secretary/treasurer with the Firefighters Burn Fund in Winnipeg and a full-time firefighter. His wife, Barbara, gave him a recipe to send. He says, "The guys at work always look forward to me bringing a jar or two of Barbara's 'Antipasto Dip' to the fire hall."

Frank M. Lucca is another firefighter from Buffalo. He has worked with Engine Company 16 for his entire 7 year career, near the War Memorial Stadium where the Buffalo Bills used to play. He sends us the "Macaroni & Peas" recipe. It's not only an inexpensive favorite at the firehouse, but is also enjoyed by his young son.

A.J. Masi is a lieutenant with the Vancouver Fire Department, serving his area for 21 years. He sends along a couple of recipes that he even receives "…the odd phone call at home" for, including his "Fettucini Alfredo" recipe.

Paul Massarelli has been a paramedic with the Baltimore County Fire Department for the past three years. Paul does most of the meal prep at his station house, and sent along "a few favorites" including a terrific "Brunch Casserole" and an innovative "Best Sauerkraut Surprise Salad". Thanks Paul.

John J. Mento is a firefighter with a hazardous material outfit in Syracuse, N.Y. He sends us his "Haz-Mat #12 Shrimp Scampi" recipe and says he has never seen an empty belly when he serves it.

Fred Mustin is a retired member of the Baltimore City Fire Department. After 30 years of service, he not only left with great memories, but a favorite chip dip recipe, which he graciously shares with us.

Brian Myroniuk, an Edmonton firefighter, sends along his recipe for "Creamy Caesar Salad," always a hit on pasta night.

Lieutenant Wayne Neeley of the Arlington, Texas Fire Department has been a firefighter for 28 years. He submits "Wayne's Sweet Tater Supreme Cake," a down-home cake with lots of sweet taters from the Lone Star State.

Jen Neubeck's husband is a Baltimore City firefighter and sent along the recipe for "Hot Milk Cake." You'll find it is one of the world's most easy and straightforward cake recipes.

Lieutenant **Ken Pardoe** is the Health and Control officer with the Anne Arundel County Fire Department, in Maryland. It is no understatement to say that without his contributions, the Beverage Chapter would be non-existent. His writing style and Health and Nutrition Newsletter are some of the best this writer has ever seen.

Craig Prusansky is a firefighter/paramedic in Palm Beach County. He is one of 800 firefighters staffing 26 fire stations. He and his two colleagues ran 1,500 calls last year. He contributed two wonderful chicken recipes, "Broiled Lemon Chicken" and "Chicken Marsala," both of which are easily executed.

Paul J. Rooney found his niche cooking in his rookie year and highly recommends his "Hall #7 Barbecued Orange Chicken." He is one of 450 firefighters among 15 fire halls. In 1992, the Scarborough, Ontario Fire Department answered about 18,000 calls.

John Schimeck, a firefighter with the Detroit Fire Department, sends along some standard firehouse fare, including a great pork roast recipe and one of two chili recipes.

Michael Schuchman is a firefighter with the Baltimore City Fire Department, Engine Company #56. He obviously loves his career as much as his wife, naming his contribution "Patti-O BBQ Sauce & Pork Ribs."

Norman J. Schwendler works at Ladder #2 in Buffalo. He has been a firefighter for 16 years and sends along several of his stations' favorite recipes.

Darlene Shedlock's husband is equally proud of his wife's famous "Four Layer Dessert" as he is of all the guys at the Baltimore City Fire Department's Engine #57.

David Veljacic is one firefighter from the City of Vancouver Fire Department of unsurpassed culinary skill. His recipes are scattered throughout the book, and most have won cooking contests across North America. I am proud to include some of David's contributions as arguably the best in the book. I am particularly fond of his "BBQ Salmon", "Fisherman's Prize" and "Award-winning Homestyle Chili" recipes.

"Classic Italian Spaghetti Sauce" comes from the "A-turn" shift at station #32 on the North side of Pittsburgh. Who says too many cooks spoil the sauce? Much thanks to **Norman Kroniser, Charles Boylan, Rich Krupa, Al Plutt and Jim Whitehouse.**

Foreword

I remember well the meals my family and I would consume, at the local volunteer fire hall. When I was a boy, in the true spirit of community, the meals were always served family-style at long banquet tables, one family astride the other. Together, we gobbled piles of homemade biscuits and mounds of mashed potatoes, and the platters of roast chicken or sliced beef seemed endless.

Born out of necessity, communal dining has become one of mankinds' most cherished of pastimes. Conversation flows as bread is broken, and ideas pass around like second helpings of rich, dark gravy. A strong sense of unity is always developed in any community, and likewise any firehouse, that cooks and eats together.

I thought this book would be a nice compliment to all the men and women in those "communities", from large city battalions, to rural volunteer outfits. For all their hard work and courage, I wanted to honor them with a book from their contemporaries around the continent. In essence, they wrote this book. While it's true, I did add some of my own recipes to aid in rounding out the chapters, I did this only after the scope and direction of the book was determined by the firefighters.

Their submissions indicated to me that firefighters invariably lean toward recipes that would appeal to the average North American. By my saying that, I realize I am saying this book is a veritable potpourri of recipes. Firehouse cooks run up and down the culinary ladder as readily as they run up and down any ladder. I would venture to say, that if you walk into nearly any firehouse that cooks you're almost certain to see Macaroni and Cheese being prepared one night, Stuffed Lamb Chops the next, and maybe Roast Woolly Mammoth on the third. However, it was obvious that firefighters generally rely on the most simple recipes, ones that can be prepared with little effort and even less time. This is probably why Casserole and Chili con Carne recipes are so popular, and why I've included two versions of the latter.

I take liberties in assuming the reader has at least a basic knowledge of rudimentary cooking and recipe-reading skills. Some recipes are quite simple, with few ingredients and few steps, while others are a bit more lengthy and might require a few "exotic" ingredients. However, none of the ingredients should be difficult to find, and any cook of moderate talent should be able to handle all the recipes with ease.

As we journey through this book, we also journey through the firehouse kitchens of North America. Thank you, ladies and gentlemen, for sharing with us your sense of brotherhood and commonality. The people of our two nations applaud the many contributions you make to our society. As our firefighters, you act as our fearless protectors, and also are the bearers of that torch called tradition.

Speaking of tradition; while I haven't made it in for dinner lately, last summer as I drove by that old firehouse I caught myself smiling. These many years later, only now with a fancier sign, that little volunteer outfit, was still encouraging people to stop the following Saturday for an "all-you-can-eat" pancake breakfast. Thinking of those stacks of fluffy pancakes from my youth, I made a promise to myself I knew I'd have no trouble keeping.

AUSPICIOUS APPETIZERS

Auspicious Appetizers

Here's the chapter that whets our appetites for all the good things to come, and I'm sure we've all been to plenty of fine parties where the assortment of tasty appetizers was the meal.

Some appetizers can be time-consuming to make, so I prefer the ones that can be made up ahead, and then quickly finished off. This way I'm almost always free to spend more time with my guests.

This chapter includes some recipes that seem to work better before you actually sit at the table, like the spreads and finger foods. Others seem better suited for service when you're actually at the table, like a small plate of the Texas Savory Grilled Shrimp or the oysters on the half shell. When choosing appetizers, I try and find one that's not too rich; one that's hot (but not necessarily spicy); and one that's chilled. Always be careful not to fill your guests up on too many of these goodies, or you'll run the risk of having lots of entree leftovers.

Many things will determine your choice of recipes. The number of guests you are serving, and the scope of the meal you wish to present are just two of them. Keeping these in mind will help you determine the variety and number of recipes you might want to prepare.

At large cocktail parties, I like to set out an assortment of cold dips, strategically placed around the room, with a variety of colorful vegetables and crisp crackers. This way the earlier guests have something to nibble on as the rest show up. It should go without saying, but always have plenty of small napkins set about anytime you're serving finger foods. You don't want to be surprised by how many your guests use.

At smaller dinner parties, I generally serve an appetizer that will compliment the entree. A rich, creamy appetizer will compliment a simple broiled lamb chop or fish quite well. In contrast, I would serve something a bit lighter, such as the ceviche, to compliment a heavier entree such as a heavy pasta or sautéed dish.

Regardless of which route you choose, remember appetizers should always be satisfying in taste, appearance, texture, and portion size. Any meal that begins with an appetizer, is almost certain to be a hit.

15

Texas Savory Grilled Shrimp

¼ cup olive oil
2 large cloves garlic, minced
  juice of 1 lemon
1 tablespoon fresh-ground black pepper
2 tablespoons minced fresh parsley
30 jumbo shrimp (don't be afraid to use the biggest you can find!)
15 slices lean bacon, remove fatty ends, and divide into halves

In a 9x13-inch baking pan, combine the olive oil, garlic, lemon juice, pepper and parsley.

Add the shrimp; toss to coat well and set aside.

Preheat your barbecue grill over a medium-high flame.

Wrap a slice of the bacon around each shrimp and fasten with a wooden pick.

Grill the shrimp for about 5 minutes, turning and basting once.

Shrimp are done when they are no longer opaque and the bacon begins to crisp.

Serve hot, individually, off a platter, or serve portions on a small bed of shredded lettuce with a dollop of hot salsa on the side and lots of fresh lemon wedges.

Serves 8–10 people

This is one versatile dish from the "Lone Star State". I serve it as a main course whenever I find really large shrimp on sale.

Crabmeat and Cheese Rolls

1   dozen fresh dinner rolls, split
¾   cup butter
1½   cups grated American cheese
3   tablespoons finely minced white onion
1   7 ounce can crabmeat, drained
      salt and fresh-ground black pepper, to taste

Arrange the roll halves onto 2 lightly buttered cookie sheets; set aside.

In a medium frying pan, melt the butter over medium heat.

Add the American cheese, onion and crabmeat.

Cook until well combined and the cheese is just melted.

Remove from heat and season with the salt and pepper.

Spread equal amounts of the mixture over the 24 dinner roll halves.

Place under a preheated broiler for 6 minutes or until the tops start to become brown and bubbly.

Cut each hot dinner roll in half.

Serve immediately.

Makes 48 hot hors d'oeuvres

This fast and tasty hors d'oeuvre should be garnished with a sprinkle of chopped chives, red pepper strips, anchovy fillets, caviar, or parsley.

Hot Spinach and Cheese Squares

★ ★ ★ ★ ★ ★ ★ ★ ★ ★ ★ ★ ★

2	eggs, slightly beaten
6	tablespoons all-purpose flour
1	10 ounce package spinach, defrosted, drained and excess water squeezed out
1	16 ounce container low-fat cottage cheese
1½	cups grated Cheddar cheese
¼	teaspoon fresh-ground black pepper
¼	teaspoon cayenne pepper
⅛	teaspoon nutmeg
3	tablespoons wheat germ

Preheat oven to 350°F, and generously grease a 9x13-inch baking pan.

In a large bowl, beat the eggs and flour until smooth.

Add the spinach, cottage cheese, Cheddar cheese, black pepper, cayenne pepper and nutmeg.

Mix until well combined.

Spoon into the prepared baking pan.

Sprinkle evenly with the wheat germ.

Bake uncovered, at 350°F for 45 minutes, or until slightly puffed and a knife inserted in the center comes out clean.

Let stand for 10 minutes before cutting into 1½-inch squares.

Makes about 48 hors d'oeuvres

Serve these as an appetizer or on the buffet table. They can be made ahead, frozen or refrigerated, and reheated for service later on.

Ceviche

★ ★ ★ ★ ★ ★ ★ ★ ★ ★ ★ ★ ★

2   pounds fresh whitefish fillets, skinless
2   large red bell peppers, peeled, seeded and chopped*
1   large red onion, diced
8   large cloves garlic, minced
½   cup fresh parsley, minced
¼   cup balsamic vinegar
½   cup olive oil
1   tablespoon fresh-ground black pepper
1   teaspoon salt
1½ cups fresh lemon juice
½   cup fresh lime juice

Rinse the fish and cut into bite-sized pieces.

In a large glass bowl, combine the fish, peppers, onion, garlic, parsley, vinegar, olive oil, black pepper, salt, lemon and lime juices; mix well.

Cover and refrigerate for at least 12 hours, or until the fish is no longer opaque and is white all the way through.

Drain and discard the liquid.

Serve the fish mixture on a bed of shredded Radicchio or Romaine lettuce with lots of lemon wedges.

* To skin the peppers, place them under the broiler until the skin "blisters" and browns. You should now be able to peel it off easily.

Serves 8–10 people

This "uncooked" fish dish is sometimes spelled "seviche." No matter—it's the same recipe. Serve it as the fish course, appetizer or salad. The acid in the lemon/lime juice is what actually "cooks" the fish. You can also try some small bay scallops or medium-size shrimp.

Oysters On The Half Shell

24 oysters, well scrubbed
8 large cloves garlic, minced
1 tablespoon salt
4 tablespoons minced fresh parsley
2 tablespoons minced sun-dried tomatoes
¼ cup olive oil
2 lemons, cut into wedges

Open the oysters with a very dull knife and discard the top shell.

Arrange the oysters in a shallow baking dish "on the half shell".

Preheat the broiler.

In a small bowl, mash the garlic and salt together with a fork.

Add the parsley, tomatoes and olive oil; mix well.

Place a heaping teaspoon of the garlic/tomato mixture on each oyster.

Broil for 10–15 minutes or until hot and bubbly.

Serve immediately with the lemon wedges.

Makes 4–6 appetizers or 24 hors d'oeuvres

These cocktail party staples are delicious, and it'll be tempting to gobble them too soon from the hot oven. Remind your guests to use care when handling the baked oyster shells— they will be very hot.

Hot Artichoke Dip

1	14 ounce can water-packed artichoke hearts, drained
½	cup sour cream
⅓	cup mayonnaise
¼	cup fresh-grated Parmesan cheese
¼	cup fresh bread crumbs
2	tablespoons butter or margarine, melted
1	tablespoon minced fresh parsley

Preheat oven to 350°F.

In a food processor or blender, puree the artichoke hearts, sour cream, mayonnaise and Parmesan cheese together.

Spoon into a small, shallow, ovenproof casserole.

In a small bowl, combine the bread crumbs, butter and parsley; mix well.

Sprinkle evenly over the artichoke heart mixture.

Bake, uncovered, at 350°F for 25 minutes, or until hot.

Makes about 3 cups

Good dippers: cooked fresh artichoke leaves, sliced large raw mushrooms, raw zucchini spears, chunks of French bread.

Party Chip Dip

1	2 pound round rye, pumpernickel or whole-wheat loaf
2	cups sour cream
1½	cups mayonnaise
2	tablespoons minced fresh parsley
2	tablespoons minced white onion
2	teaspoons seasoning salt
2	teaspoons dried dill

Remove the top off the loaf and gently remove the bread in bite-sized pieces from inside so as to leave a large cavity.

In a large bowl, combine all remaining ingredients; mix until smooth.

Spoon the mixture into the bread cavity.

Makes about 3½ cups

Good dippers: the bread pieces, carrot sticks, celery sticks, red or green bell pepper slices, or any fresh raw vegetable.

Chunky Antipasto Dip

4	tablespoons olive oil
2	medium red bell peppers, diced small
4	medium green bell peppers, diced small
2	6 ounce cans mushroom pieces, drained
1	cup sweet relish
3	large cloves garlic, minced
½	cup white vinegar
¼	cup firmly-packed light brown sugar
¼	teaspoon cinnamon
1	7 ounce can water-packed tuna, drained and flaked
12	green olives, sliced thin
1½	cups catsup
1	7 ounce can tiny shrimp, drained
12	ripe black olives, sliced thin
1½	cups prepared chili sauce
½	head cauliflower, cut into small flowerets

In a large saucepan, heat the olive oil over low heat.

Add the red and green bell peppers; sauté until soft.

Add the mushrooms, relish, garlic, vinegar, brown sugar and cinnamon.

Increase the heat to high, and bring to a boil, stirring constantly.

Reduce heat to simmer, and add all remaining ingredients; mix well.

Cover and simmer for 1 hour, stirring occasionally.

Store in the refrigerator, in well-sealed jars, for up to 3 weeks.

Serve on crackers, bread, taco chips, or lettuce.

Makes about 1 quart of antipasto dip

Good dippers: taco chips, crackers, bread or lettuce. Perfect for football, either at the stadium, or at the television.

Smoked Salmon Dip

1   8 ounce package cream cheese, softened
⅓   cup milk
5   ounces sliced smoked salmon, cut into pieces
2   tablespoons fresh lemon juice
1   tablespoon dried dill

In a food processor or blender, puree all the ingredients until very smooth.

Cover and chill at least 1 hour.

Makes about 1½ cups

Good dippers: toasted bagel chips, wedges of thin pumpernickel, Belgian endive spears, sugar snap or snow peas.

Tofu-Peanut Dip

8   ounces drained firm tofu (bean curd)
⅓   cup sour cream
¼   cup creamy peanut butter
3   tablespoons milk
1   tablespoon sesame oil
1   tablespoon red wine vinegar
2   teaspoons soy sauce
¼   teaspoon ground ginger

In a food processor or blender, puree all the ingredients until very smooth.

Cover and chill at least 1 hour.

Makes about 1¾ cups

Good dippers: canned baby corn, water chestnuts, snow peas or sugar snap peas, toasted pita pocket wedges.

23

Pesto Dip

3 cups loosely packed fresh basil leaves
2 teaspoons minced garlic
½ cup olive oil
½ cup walnut pieces
1 cup low-fat cottage cheese
½ cup fresh-grated Parmesan cheese
⅓ cup fresh lemon juice
½ teaspoon salt

In a food processor or blender, puree the basil leaves, garlic, olive oil and walnut pieces together.

Add the cottage cheese, Parmesan cheese, lemon juice and salt.

Process until very smooth, and creamy.

Cover and chill at least 1 hour.

Makes about 2½ cups

Good dippers: cherry tomatoes, cheese strips, chilled cooked tortellini, chunks of cold meatloaf.

Tonnato Dip

1　7 ounce can water-packed tuna, drained
4　flat anchovy fillets
3　tablespoons fresh lemon juice
1　cup mayonnaise
2　tablespoons chicken broth or water
2　tablespoons capers, drained

In a food processor or blender, puree the tuna, anchovy fillets, and lemon juice together.

Add the mayonnaise, chicken broth or water, and capers.

Process just until blended and creamy.

Cover and chill at least 1 hour.

Makes about 1½ cups

Good dippers: large, sliced mushrooms, pumpernickel or rye bread rounds, Belgian endive or romaine lettuce spears.

Garlic-Potato Dip

2　cups prepared instant, or homemade, mashed potatoes
　　(made without butter or salt)
1　tablespoon minced garlic
½　teaspoon salt
½　cup olive oil
¼　cup red wine vinegar
¼　cup water

In a food processor or blender, puree the mashed potatoes, garlic and salt.

In a small bowl, combine the olive oil, vinegar and water.

With the machine running, slowly add the liquid mixture in a slow, steady stream.

Process until very smooth.

Cover and chill at least 1 hour.

Makes about 3 cups

Good dippers: hot crunchy fish sticks, French-fried onion rings, sliced or whole cooked baby beets, fried Kielbasa or other sausage.

Pinto Bean Dip

1	16 ounce can pinto beans, rinsed and drained
4	small green onions, chopped fine
3	tablespoons olive oil
2	tablespoons lemon juice
2	tablespoons water
1	tablespoon minced fresh parsley
1	teaspoon minced garlic
½	teaspoon salt

In a food processor or blender, puree all ingredients until very smooth.

Cover and chill at least 1 hour.

Makes about 2½ cups

Good dippers: large corn tortilla chips, celery sticks, avocado chunks or sliced red bell pepper.

Creamy Curry Dip

1	cup mayonnaise
1	cup sour cream
2	tablespoons fresh lime juice
1	tablespoon curry powder
½	teaspoon salt

In a medium bowl, combine all ingredients.

Blend well with a wire whisk until smooth.

Cover and chill at least 1 hour.

Makes about 2 cups

Good dippers: red and green seedless grapes, apple wedges, chilled shrimp, cold cubes of cooked ham, turkey or chicken.

SUPERB SOUPS

SOUPS

Superb Soups

This chapter deals with what many consider a starter, or first course. But some of these simple and hearty soups are actually meals and I've tried to offer some serving suggestions that help make them part of a balanced meal.

Some of the soups included in this chapter are considered the mainstays of North American kitchens, like the Lentil-Ham Soup, and some are old favorites with a new twist, like the Pumpkin Soup spiced with curry. You'll find the Shrimp Gumbo recipe in the Main Course chapter, and one of the most ethnic is the Italian Tortellini Soup. This offering is very good, but don't leave it on the stove too long, or the pasta will become overcooked and soggy. And remember, be careful not to boil the cream soups after the milk products are added, or you'll run the risk of curdling.

Soup is generally one of those dishes that improve with long, slow simmering. Perhaps the largest pitfall many new soup cooks experience is being a bit too heavy-handed with the seasonings. Because the long simmering time will evaporate some of the liquid, and concentrate the seasoning flavors; your finished product might be a bit too salty or taste over-seasoned. You can help avoid this problem by under-spicing during preparation, and adjusting the spices and flavorings an hour or so before service.

Because it is prepared well in advance, soup is a remarkably practical dish for both the firehouse cook and the homemaker. Soup recipes allow the cook to use all sorts of leftovers, and by skillfully combining ingredients, the cook can experiment with a great number of tastes, textures, and flavorings. Be creative and show ingenuity. The variety of ingredients that can be used are limitless, and in reality, there is no edible material that can not be used in its preparation. You can always change the ingredient amounts to scale them up or down, depending on how many people you have to serve, and how big their appetites are.

DV's Clam Chowder

2½ pounds white potatoes, unpeeled
½ pound bacon, chopped fine
3 large leeks, diced
1 cup diced celery
5 large okra, diced
3 cups water
2 cups clam juice
2 cups minced clams, drained, reserve the liquid
2½ cups chopped clams, drained, reserve the liquid
1 cup heavy cream
1 tablespoon fresh-ground black pepper
1 medium carrot, grated
salt, to taste
milk

In a large sauce pan, cover the scrubbed and unpeeled potatoes with water and simmer until almost done (about 20 minutes).

Drain, cool, and peel the potatoes.

Cube the potatoes into ½-inch squares and set aside.

In a large sauce pan, fry the bacon until crisp; remove with a slotted spoon and drain on paper towelling.

Sauté the leeks, celery, and okra in the bacon fat over medium heat until soft.

Add the water and simmer until most of the liquid is gone (about 10 minutes).

In a food processor or blender, puree the leeks, celery, and okra with the clam juice and reserved clam liquid.

In the sauce pan, combine the minced and chopped clams, the vegetable puree, potato cubes, bacon and cream, over medium-high heat.

Reduce heat and add the pepper, cover and simmer for 15 minutes, stirring occasionally.

Add the carrot and simmer 15 minutes more.

Thin as necessary with the milk.

Makes about 3 quarts

This is just the soup for those chilly, early fall, Friday nights. It's a must to serve this with salty oyster crackers and a fresh green garden salad on the side.

Crab Bisque

2	packets instant chicken soup mix
2	cups hot water
2	tablespoons butter or margarine
2	tablespoons all-purpose flour
2	large cloves garlic, minced
2	tablespoons minced fresh parsley
2	cups evaporated skim milk
½	teaspoon cayenne pepper
½	teaspoon nutmeg
2	7 ounce cans crabmeat
3	tablespoons sherry

Dissolve the soup mix in the hot water and set aside.

In a medium sauce pan, melt the butter over medium heat.

Add the flour, garlic and parsley.

Sauté lightly.

Slowly stir in the chicken soup mixture.

Cook, stirring constantly, until thickened.

Stir in all the remaining ingredients (except the wine).

Reduce heat and cook over low heat, stirring frequently, until thoroughly heated.

Stir in the sherry.

Remove from heat and serve hot in warmed bowls.

Makes about ½ quart

Serve with crusty French bread and whipped butter. It compliments a fresh fruit salad and cheese platter marvelously.

Conch Chowder

2   large conches, rinsed
2   medium onions, chopped fine
1   green bell pepper, chopped fine
¼   pound salt pork, chopped fine
1   6 ounce can tomato paste
4   cups hot water
1   bay leaf
2   large cloves garlic, minced
1   tablespoon barbecue sauce
½   tablespoon poultry seasoning
½   teaspoon oregano
½   teaspoon fresh-ground black pepper
¾   teaspoon salt
1   pound potatoes, pared and diced large

Pound the conches to break up the tissue and chop them into small pieces; set aside.

In a large sauce pan, sauté the onion, bell pepper and salt pork, over medium-high heat, until the onion is soft and transparent.

Add all of the other ingredients (except conches and potatoes).

Bring to a slow boil, stirring often.

Add the conch pieces.

Reduce heat and cover, simmer slowly for 2 hours, stirring occasionally.

Add the potatoes and simmer for 30 minutes more, or until done.

Remove bay leaf and serve hot in warmed bowls.

Makes about 2 quarts

A conch, pronounced "konk," is a large mollusk. This chowder version is considered quite a delicacy up and down the Florida Keys. While it might not be easy to get everywhere in the country, ask at your local fish market. If they don't have it, see if they can order it. This is one of my oldest firehouse recipes and I cherish it.

Cheese and Vegetable Chowder

3 tablespoons butter or margarine
1½ cups chopped celery
1 cup grated carrot
2 small green onions, sliced and separated into rings
2 10 ounce cans cream of potato soup
1 14 ounce can chicken broth
½ cup water
2 tablespoons minced fresh parsley
2 dashes hot red pepper sauce
2 cups (8 ounces) grated Cheddar or Colby cheese
1 13 ounce can evaporated milk
3 tablespoons sherry

In a large sauce pan, melt the butter over medium-high heat.

Add the celery, carrot and onion.

Cook until tender, but do not brown.

Add the potato soup, chicken broth, water, parsley and red pepper sauce.

Cook, stirring constantly, until boiling.

Reduce heat and cover, simmer for 20 minutes, stirring occasionally.

Stir in the cheese, evaporated milk and sherry.

Reheat gently, but do not boil, stirring constantly until the cheese melts.

Serve immediately.

Makes about 1 quart

Serve hot in warmed bowls with a basket of oyster crackers for a satisfying hot lunch or late supper.

Curried Pumpkin Soup

★ ★ ★ ★ ★ ★ ★ ★ ★ ★ ★ ★ ★

¼	cup butter or margarine
1	medium onion, coarsely chopped
1	large clove garlic, minced
1	16 ounce can solid-pack pumpkin
4	teaspoons curry powder
¼	teaspoon salt
¼	teaspoon fresh-ground black pepper
¼	teaspoon sugar
¼	teaspoon nutmeg
1	bay leaf
4	cups chicken broth
2	cups milk
½	cup shredded, unsweetened, toasted coconut

In a large sauce pan, melt the butter over medium heat.

Add the onion and garlic; sauté until very soft (about 5 minutes).

Stir in the pumpkin, curry powder, salt, pepper, sugar, nutmeg and bay leaf.

Pour in the broth and bring to a boil, stirring often.

Reduce heat and simmer for 30 minutes.

Remove from heat and discard bay leaf.

Stir in the milk.

Reheat gently, making sure not to boil.

Serve hot in warmed bowls.

Garnish with the toasted coconut.

Makes about 1 quart

This is THE harvest soup, spiced with the curry it becomes something exotic. For a fast October meal, it compliments almost any casserole with a taste of the season.

Winter Vegetable Soup

★ ★ ★ ★ ★ ★ ★ ★ ★ ★ ★ ★ ★

7	cups water
3	medium white turnips (about ¾ pound), pared and cut into bite-size pieces
1	large red onion, chopped (about 1 cup)
1	large yellow onion, chopped (about 1 cup)
2	large potatoes (about 1 pound), cut into large chunks
7	carrots, sliced into ¼-inch thick rounds (about 2 cups)
½	small rutabaga, pared and chopped (about 1 cup)
2	medium beets, unpeeled, well scrubbed, and cut into small cubes
¾	cup sliced scallions, with the tops
1	large clove garlic, minced
2	tablespoons minced fresh parsley
1	tablespoon basil
2	teaspoons salt
½	teaspoon fresh-ground black pepper
2	tablespoons butter or margarine
1	tablespoon dried chives

In a large sauce pan, combine the water, turnips, red and yellow onions over high heat.

Bring to a boil, reduce heat, and cover.

Simmer, stirring occasionally, for about 45 minutes, or until the vegetables become very soft.

Add the potatoes, carrots, and rutabaga.

Simmer, covered, for 15 minutes more, or until the potatoes are barely tender.

Add the beets, green onions, garlic, parsley, basil, salt and pepper.

Simmer, covered, until beets are tender, about 15–20 minutes (the soup will be pink).

Remove from heat, and stir in the butter and chives.

Serve hot in warmed bowls.

Garnish with a dollop of sour cream, if you wish.

Makes about 1½ quarts

Don't let the red color scare you, this is a must-try vegetable soup with a twist. A tried and true recipe from a small volunteer outfit in northern Minnesota, and they know something about winter!

Lentil-Ham Soup

3   tablespoons vegetable oil
1½   cups sliced carrots
1   cup diced celery
¾   cup diced onion
2   cups cubed cooked ham
½   teaspoon thyme
2   bay leaves
1   teaspoon salt
¼   teaspoon fresh-ground black pepper
1   16 ounce can whole tomatoes, chopped, reserve the liquid
7   cups water
1   16 ounce package dried lentils
¼   cup minced fresh parsley

In a large sauce pan, heat the oil over medium heat.

Add the carrots, celery and onion.

Cook, stirring occasionally, for about 10 minutes, or until the onion is slightly brown.

Add the ham, thyme, bay leaves, salt, pepper, tomatoes, their juice, water and lentils.

Bring to a slow boil, stirring often.

Reduce heat and cover, simmer for about 50 minutes, or until the lentils are tender.

Stir in the parsley.

Remove the bay leaves.

Serve hot in warmed bowls.

Makes about 2 quarts

This is one of those fantastic soups that keeps great on the stove all day for whenever someone is hungry. Make sure you have lots of crackers and chewy whole-grain bread on hand, and you can feel satisfied that you are providing a very healthy, hearty snack.

Turkey Vegetable Soup

1 pound ground turkey
1 16 ounce can whole tomatoes, chopped, reserve the liquid
1 8 ounce can tomato sauce
1 cup chopped red onion
1 cup diced raw potato, peeled
1 cup chopped cabbage
1 cup diced green bell pepper
1 10 ounce package frozen green beans
1 10 ounce package frozen whole-kernel corn
1 10 ounce package frozen peas
½ cup thinly sliced carrots
1 bay leaf
½ teaspoon basil
¼ teaspoon fresh-ground black pepper
¼ teaspoon thyme
½ teaspoon garlic powder
6 cups water

In a large sauce pan, brown the turkey meat, over medium heat.

Add the tomatoes, their liquid, tomato sauce, onion, potatoes, cabbage, green bell pepper, green beans, corn, peas, carrots, bay leaf, basil, pepper, thyme, garlic powder and water.

Bring to a slow boil, stirring often.

Reduce heat and cover, simmer for about 1 hour, or until the vegetables are tender, stirring occasionally.

Remove the bay leaf and serve hot in warmed bowls with crusty Italian bread.

Makes about 1½ quarts

This nutritious soup, low in sodium and low in fat, is just the thing to take the chill out of the early nights of January.

Italian Tortellini Soup

4   14 ounce cans beef broth
4   cups water
1   pound sweet Italian sausage, cut into ½-inch pieces
1   9 ounce box frozen cheese tortellini
1   9 ounce box frozen spinach tortellini
2   cups grated cabbage
1   small green bell pepper, cored and diced
1   medium zucchini, unpeeled and sliced thin
1   small red onion, chopped
1   medium fresh tomato, diced
1   tablespoon chopped fresh basil
    salt and fresh-ground black pepper, to taste
    fresh-grated Parmesan cheese

In a large sauce pan, combine the beef broth, water, Italian sausage, both boxes of tortellini, cabbage, bell pepper, zucchini, onion, tomato and basil.

Bring to a slow boil, over medium-high heat.

Reduce heat and simmer, loosely covered, for 15–20 minutes, or until the vegetables are tender.

Season with the salt and pepper.

Serve hot in warmed bowls, with a sprinkle of Parmesan cheese.

Makes about 5 quarts, but halves easily

This recipe comes from Philadelphia, and is great served with crusty garlic bread. It's especially good the next day, when reheated from the refrigerator.

SAVORY SALADS
AND
DELECTABLE DRESSINGS

★ ★ ★ ★ ★ ★ ★ ★ ★ ★ ★ ★ ★

★ ★ ★ ★ ★ ★ ★ ★ ★ ★ ★ ★ ★

★ ★ ★ ★ ★ ★ ★ ★ ★ ★ ★ ★ ★

Savory Salads and Dressings

★ ★ ★ ★ ★ ★ ★ ★ ★ ★ ★ ★ ★

Most all of us grew up eating the salads our mothers made for us before we could start slicing up Thursday Baked Lasagna or Tuesday Pot Roast. Every evening, promptly at 6, my family would gather around our kitchen table. Mom, with the usual tossed green salad, in the big wooden bowl with the chip. Piling mountains of crisp iceberg lettuce, tossed with only carrot, celery, onion and maybe some tomato wedges (if they were in season) onto our plates, she would order one of us kids to get the assortment of dressings from the refrigerator. And order the rest of us to stop arguing and start eating. Long before the researchers told her, she knew how important it was that her family eat "their daily allowance".

Salads have become much more sophisticated now, but the concept is still the same, fresh crisp greens, hearty, flavorful vegetables and a properly seasoned dressing.

Many salads in this chapter are considered to be starter, or first coarse salads, like the refreshing Tomato/Onion Salad or the Creamy Caesar Salad. Some are considered accompaniment salads, like the spicy Curried Potato Salad or the cool Tropical Cole Slaw. Still others are hot, main course salads, like the Berkeley Meatball Salad or the Hot Chicken-Citrus Salad. And some, like the Kiwi-Melon Salad, you might want to consider as a light lunch salad or for a brunch buffet table. And for a crunchy and hearty vegetable salad, try either the tasty Carrot Salad or the Broccoli and Peanut Salad.

From Nova Scotia to Tijuana, these tried and true recipes have graced many a barbecue buffet or winter potluck dinner table. Of course, all the recipes in this chapter can be altered to give appropriate serving sizes to suit whichever use you have for them, whether it be to serve a full house of twenty or a small contingent of close friends.

Tomato/Onion Salad

6	large cloves garlic, minced
½	teaspoon salt
¼	teaspoon coriander
1	cup olive oil
1	tablespoon fresh-ground black pepper
¼	cup balsamic vinegar
¼	cup minced fresh basil
6	large fresh tomatoes, sliced ⅛-inch thick
2	large purple or Bermuda onions, sliced into thin rings and separated
1	small head Iceberg lettuce, shredded

In a large bowl, mash the garlic and salt together with a fork.

Add the coriander, olive oil, pepper, vinegar and basil.

Mix well.

Place the tomatoes and onions into the dressing and gently toss to coat evenly.

Cover tightly and refrigerate overnight, tossing occasionally.

Serve individual portions with a slotted spoon on a bed of shredded lettuce.

Serves 6–8 people

I always substitute Vidalias for Bermuda onions, when they're in season. Fresh, ripe garden tomatoes and fresh garden basil are a must for this refreshing summer salad from a friend in Vancouver, B.C.

Radicchio/Endive Salad

1	medium head Radicchio lettuce, rinsed and well drained
2	medium heads Belgian endive, rinsed and well drained
½	teaspoon sugar
3	tablespoons olive oil
½	teaspoon fresh-ground black pepper
2	teaspoons white vinegar
2	teaspoons balsamic vinegar
1	teaspoon minced fresh parsley

In a large bowl, tear the Radicchio and Belgian endive into bite-size pieces.

Toss together lightly.

In a small bowl, combine the sugar, olive oil, pepper, white and balsamic vinegars; mix well.

Pour over the lettuce and toss well to coat all the leaves.

Garnish with a sprinkle of the parsley.

Serve immediately on cold plates.

Serves 6 people

This quick salad has just what it takes to be used with all those meals that should be served with a fresh green salad. The two lettuces compliment each other especially well, and the simple dressing heightens their flavors without overpowering them.

Creamy Caesar Salad

★ ★ ★ ★ ★ ★ ★ ★ ★ ★ ★ ★ ★

2	medium heads Romaine lettuce, rinsed and drained well
1	small tin anchovy fillets, minced fine
3	cups freshly-made Italian bread croutons
¾	cup sunflower oil
5	large cloves garlic, minced
1½	teaspoons dry mustard
½	teaspoon salt
¾	teaspoon fresh-ground black pepper
¾	teaspoon Worcestershire sauce
1	tablespoon white wine vinegar
2	tablespoons fresh lemon juice
¼	cup fresh-grated Parmesan cheese
2	tablespoons cream cheese, softened
2	egg yolks, coddled

In a large bowl, place the lettuce and tear it into small bite-size pieces.

Add the anchovies and croutons; toss well, and set aside.

In a blender container, combine the sunflower oil, garlic, mustard, salt, pepper, Worcestershire sauce, vinegar and lemon juice.

Blend until completely combined.

Add the Parmesan cheese, cream cheese and egg yolks.

Blend again until completely combined.

Pour the dressing over the lettuce, anchovies and croutons.

Toss to coat well.

Garnish with more grated Parmesan cheese.

Serve immediately on cold plates.

Serves 8–10 people

To coddle the eggs, place the entire egg in very hot water and let it sit for 1 minute, then being very careful, crack the egg and separate the yolk from the white.

This is an easy variation on one of the continent's most beloved of salads.

44

Carrot Salad

★ ★ ★ ★ ★ ★ ★ ★ ★ ★ ★ ★ ★

5	cups sliced carrots
1	large white onion, sliced and separated into thin rings
1	cup diced red bell pepper
1	cup diced green bell pepper
1	10 ounce can tomato soup
2	tablespoons catsup
½	cup salad oil
¼	cup sugar
1	teaspoon salt
1	teaspoon fresh-ground black pepper
1	4 ounce can button mushrooms, drained
1	tablespoon minced fresh parsley

Cook the carrots 3–4 minutes, in 1 quart of rapidly boiling water (they should still be quite crunchy and not too soft).

Drain the carrots and cool quickly in an ice water bath (this stops the cooking process).

In a large bowl, combine the drained carrots, onion and bell peppers.

In a medium bowl, combine the tomato soup, catsup, oil, sugar, salt and pepper; mix well.

Pour over the carrot mixture, and toss until all the ingredients are well coated.

Cover tightly and refrigerate overnight.

At service time, add the button mushrooms and toss again.

Garnish with a sprinkle of the fresh parsley.

Serve immediately.

Serves 8–10 people

As everyone knows, lots of carrots help us see better in the dark. They're tasty in this salad that is wonderful on all kinds of buffet tables—from the Fourth of July, to the office Christmas party.

Broccoli and Peanut Salad

★ ★ ★ ★ ★ ★ ★ ★ ★ ★ ★ ★ ★

2	medium bunches fresh broccoli, cut into flowerets (about 5 cups)
1	small red onion, diced
1	cup red Spanish peanuts, salted
½	cup dark raisins
1	cup mayonnaise
½	cup sugar
2	tablespoons red wine vinegar

In a large bowl, combine the broccoli, onion, peanuts and raisins.

Mix well.

Cover and refrigerate for at least 1 hour.

At service time; in a small bowl, combine the mayonnaise, sugar and vinegar.

Mix well.

Pour the dressing over the broccoli mixture.

Mix and toss until well coated.

Serve immediately on cold plates.

Serves 4–6 people

This recipe came from Barbara in Palm Beach County. She got it from her step-mom, who got it from her beautician; where she got it "…no one knows. But the recipe is splendid. Very tasty and crunchy." I agree.

Tropical Cole Slaw

2   cups shredded cabbage
½   cup grated carrot
½   cup diced green bell pepper
1   cup crushed pineapple, well drained
1   teaspoon salt
¼   teaspoon fresh-ground black pepper
½   cup sour cream
1   large ripe banana
     dash paprika

In a large bowl, combine the cabbage, carrot, green pepper, pineapple, salt and pepper.

Add the sour cream and mix lightly.

Cover and chill at least 2–3 hours.

At service time, peel and dice the banana.

Fold into the cabbage mixture.

Garnish with paprika.

Serve immediately on cold plates.

Serves 6 people

Make sure you use a fully ripe banana (a deep-yellow peel flecked with brown). This is a great way to make something different out of a fish fry mainstay I've seen many a "cole slaw hater" go for second helpings.

Best Sauerkraut Surprise Salad

4	cups canned sauerkraut, drained well
½	cup apple cider vinegar
½	cup salad oil
1	cup finely chopped celery
¾	cup finely chopped white onion
1	cup sweet pickle relish
1	cup diced green bell pepper
1	4 ounce jar pimientos, drained and chopped
1	tablespoon celery seed
1	cup sugar

In a large bowl, place all the ingredients in the given order.

Mix thoroughly.

Cover tightly, and refrigerate for at least 8 hours.

Serve cold on cold plates.

Serves about 8 people

This is <u>classic</u> barbecue fare.

Curried Potato Salad

★ ★ ★ ★ ★ ★ ★ ★ ★ ★ ★ ★ ★

5 medium potatoes
1½ cups cooked, cut green beans
1 8 ounce container plain yogurt
1½ teaspoons salt
1 teaspoon curry powder
¼ teaspoon garlic powder
¼ teaspoon ground white pepper
½ teaspoon turmeric

In a large sauce pan, cover the potatoes with water.

Heat to boiling over high heat.

Reduce heat and simmer until the potatoes are tender when pierced with a fork.

Drain and rinse under cold water.

Peel the potatoes, and cut them into ½-inch cubes (makes about 5 cups).

In a large bowl, toss the potatoes and green beans together.

In a medium bowl, combine the yogurt, salt, curry powder, garlic powder, white pepper and turmeric together; mix well.

Pour over the potatoes and green beans.

Toss gently to coat evenly.

Cover and refrigerate at least 1 hour.

Serve chilled on cold plates.

Serves 8–10 people

Another curry dish for those who like their foods spicy. Try this recipe with your next roast chicken dinner.

Spicy Rice Salad

1 cup long grain white rice, uncooked
6 tablespoons olive oil
3 tablespoons white wine vinegar
1 teaspoon salt
1 teaspoon fresh-ground black pepper
½ teaspoon tarragon
¼ cup diced green bell pepper
¼ cup chopped fresh parsley
¼ cup chopped chives
½ cup cucumber, cut into small cubes
¼ cup chopped green onion
2 hard-cooked eggs, sliced
2 pimientos, sliced

Cook the rice according to package instructions.

After the rice has cooked, mix it at once with the olive oil, vinegar, salt, pepper and tarragon.

Let the rice mixture stand to cool.

Add the green bell pepper, parsley, chives, cucumber and chopped green onion; mix well.

Heap on greens of your choice, and garnish with slices of the hard cooked egg and pimiento strips.

Serve immediately on cold plates.

Serves 4 people

This cold rice salad works well at lunches and late suppers. Try it the next time you make chicken or seafood kebobs.

Kiwi Fruit Melon Salad

★ ★ ★ ★ ★ ★ ★ ★ ★ ★ ★ ★ ★

$\frac{3}{4}$ cup mayonnaise
2 tablespoons sugar
3 tablespoons fresh squeezed lemon juice
$\frac{1}{3}$ cup shredded sweetened coconut
$\frac{1}{2}$ teaspoon salt
1 cup honeydew melon balls
1 cup cantaloupe balls
1 cup watermelon balls
4 kiwi fruit, peeled and sliced
$\frac{1}{2}$ cup chopped walnuts

In a large bowl, combine the mayonnaise, sugar, lemon juice, coconut and salt.

Mix very well.

Gently add the kiwi fruit and melon balls to the mayonnaise mixture.

Toss lightly to coat evenly.

Cover tightly and refrigerate until well chilled.

Serve immediately, on cold plates, sprinkled with a bit of the chopped walnuts.

Serves about 6 people

You don't have to be fancy making the melon balls, you can also cut the flesh into bite-size pieces for a quick, refreshing, summertime salad. You can easily double or triple this recipe and pass it around at a friend's potluck supper.

Hot Chicken Citrus Salad

★ ★ ★ ★ ★ ★ ★ ★ ★ ★ ★ ★ ★ ★

2 cups cooked, diced chicken
1 cup diagonally sliced celery
¼ cup chopped walnuts
2 tablespoons grated white onion
½ teaspoon salt
¼ teaspoon tarragon
⅓ cup orange juice
¼ cup mayonnaise
2 oranges, peeled and sectioned
¼ cup dry bread crumbs
¼ cup fresh-grated Parmesan or Romano cheese

Lightly butter an 8x8-inch baking pan and set aside.

In a medium bowl, combine the chicken, celery, walnuts, onion, salt, tarragon, orange juice and mayonnaise; mix well.

Cover and refrigerate for at least 1 hour.

Stir in the orange sections.

Spoon mixture into the prepared baking pan.

Sprinkle with the bread crumbs and Parmesan cheese.

Bake, uncovered, in a preheated 350°F oven for 20–25 minutes, or until mixture is heated through and cheese is lightly browned.

Serve portions immediately on a bed of shredded lettuce.

Serves 4 people

This makes a hearty meal for lunch between friends and easily doubles or triples when the house is full.

Chicken Salad

3 cups cooked, diced chicken
1 cup diced celery
½ cup diced white onion
2 hard-cooked eggs, sliced
6 stuffed green olives, sliced
1 teaspoon salt
½ teaspoon fresh-ground black pepper
¼ cup mayonnaise

In a medium bowl, combine the chicken, celery, onion, eggs, olives, salt and pepper; mix well.

Add the mayonnaise 1 tablespoon at a time.

Stir just until the mixture is moistened.

Cover and chill thoroughly.

Serve chilled on salad greens or as a sandwich filler.

Serves 4–6 people

Cooked, diced veal may be used in place of all or part of the chicken to give this old deli standard an uptown flavor.

Berkeley Meatball Salad

1	pound lean ground beef
½	cup regular wheat germ
½	cup minced white onion
¼	cup catsup
1	egg, slightly beaten
1	teaspoon chili powder
½	teaspoon ground cumin
½	teaspoon salt
½	teaspoon fresh-ground black pepper
1	medium head iceberg lettuce or other greens, rinsed, drained and torn into bite-size pieces
2	medium fresh tomatoes, cut into wedges
1	small green bell pepper, cut into thin strips
½	cup pitted ripe black olives, cut into wedges
1	small green onion, sliced thin and separated into rings
½	cup olive oil
¼	cup red wine vinegar
¾	teaspoon marjoram
½	teaspoon garlic salt

Preheat oven to 400°F.

In a large bowl, combine the ground beef, wheat germ, onion, catsup, egg, chili powder, cumin, salt and pepper; mix well.

Shape the mixture into 36 small balls.

Place in an ungreased shallow baking pan.

Bake, uncovered, at 400°F for 10–12 minutes, or until evenly browned and fully cooked.

While the meatballs bake, place the lettuce pieces in a large salad bowl.

Arrange the tomatoes, green pepper and olives around the edge.

Place the cooked meatballs in the center of the salad.

Sprinkle with the green onion.

In a small bowl, combine the oil, vinegar, marjoram and garlic salt; mix well.

Pour evenly over the salad, and serve immediately.

Serves 6 people

Leave it to the Californians to put an entire meal into one course, and do it with such tasty creativity.

Florida French Dressing

2	teaspoons cornstarch
1	teaspoon sugar
¾	teaspoon salt
½	teaspoon paprika
½	teaspoon dry mustard
1	cup fresh grapefruit juice
2	tablespoons salad oil
¼	teaspoon fresh-ground black pepper
¼	cup catsup

In a small sauce pan, combine the cornstarch, sugar, salt, paprika, and dry mustard.

Mix well.

Slowly stir in the grapefruit juice.

Place over medium heat and bring to a boil, stirring constantly.

Boil 1 minute.

Remove from heat.

Stir in the salad oil, pepper, and catsup.

Cover and chill.

Mix well before serving.

Makes about 1¼ cups

Tangy Yogurt Dressing

1	cup plain yogurt
2	tablespoons canned pear syrup
2	tablespoons minced green onion
1	teaspoon Dijon mustard
¼	teaspoon salt
	dash fresh-ground black pepper

In a small bowl, combine all the ingredients.

Mix very well with a wire whisk.

Cover and chill.

Mix well before serving.

Makes about 1¼ cups

Blue Cheese Dressing

½	cup sour cream
⅓	cup crumbled blue cheese
2	tablespoons mayonnaise
2	teaspoons fresh lemon juice
½	teaspoon seasoned salt

In a small bowl, combine all the ingredients.

Mix very well with a wire whisk.

Cover and chill.

Mix well before serving.

Makes about 1 cup

Creamy Honey Dressing

½   cup mayonnaise
½   cup sour cream
2   tablespoons fresh lemon juice
1   tablespoon honey
1   tablespoon milk
½   teaspoon salad or sesame oil

In a small bowl, combine all the ingredients.

Mix very well with a wire whisk.

Cover and chill.

Mix well before serving.

Makes about 1¼ cup

Lemon Sesame Dressing

⅔   cup salad oil
3   tablespoons fresh lemon juice
2   tablespoons white wine vinegar
2   tablespoons toasted sesame seeds
1   tablespoon sugar
½   teaspoon salt

In a small bowl, combine all the ingredients.

Mix very well with a wire whisk.

Cover and chill.

Mix well before serving.

Makes about 1 cup

Garlic Vinaigrette

½   cup olive oil
2   tablespoons red wine vinegar
1   teaspoon salt
½   teaspoon fresh-ground black pepper
2   large cloves garlic, finely minced

In a small bowl, combine all the ingredients.

Mix very well with a wire whisk.

Cover and chill.

Mix well before serving.

Makes about ¾ cup

Dill Curry Dressing

1   cup salad oil
⅓   cup white wine vinegar
1   teaspoon paprika
2   teaspoons curry powder
¼   teaspoon hot red pepper sauce
¼   teaspoon Worcestershire sauce
½   teaspoon dried dill
½   teaspoon sugar

In a small bowl, combine all the ingredients.

Mix very well with a wire whisk.

Cover and chill.

Mix well before serving.

Makes about 1½ cups

MESMERIZING MAIN COURSES

★ ★ ★ ★ ★ ★ ★ ★ ★ ★ ★ ★ ★

★ ★ ★ ★ ★ ★ ★ ★ ★ ★ ★ ★ ★

Mesmerizing Main Courses

"Meat and potatoes, and lots of chili recipes." That's all I heard when I started this venture. But I had faith in the men and women out there. While I did get my share of those recipes, I also received many more recipes that mirrored the variety of the contributors.

This large chapter encompasses the vast and varied main course category. I've organized it loosely into sub-chapters: Beef, Poultry, Seafood, Pasta, and Casseroles. You'll find casseroles elsewhere in the book, but the recipes in this chapter seem appropriate for serving as the entree.

I've included some firehouse standards, like a good pork roast, and two kinds of chili. I've also included some slightly fancier fare, like "Shirred Beef with Mushrooms" or "Company Chicken." I was pleased to receive many fine seafood dishes as well, and as a great source of low-cholesterol protein I recommend the "Chinese Halibut Broil" or "Picante Fillets". If cholesterol is not an issue, and large appetites are, I suggest you try "Fisherman's Prize" for an impressive meal with a visual and tasty presentation.

In addition to the chili recipes, I've also included some other great, one-pot dishes like the "Classic Italian Spaghetti Sauce" or "Vegetarian Red Sauce." You'll notice that they are mostly simple recipes, so don't be bashful about adding some of your own favorite ingredients or seasonings. What's especially nice about these dishes is that they keep wonderfully in the pot all day (over very low heat), so that everyone can help themselves.

Some of the recipes may sound a little time consuming, but you'll notice that in most cases they can be prepared early in the day, or even the day ahead, and heated quickly for eating.

Patti-O BBQ Sauce & Pork Ribs

2–3 pounds pork spare ribs
1½ cups catsup
1 cup water
½ cup white vinegar
3 tablespoons firmly-packed brown sugar
4 teaspoons dry mustard
3 teaspoons paprika
3 tablespoons Worcestershire sauce
2 large cloves garlic, minced
3 teaspoons chili powder
1 teaspoon salt
½ teaspoon fresh-ground black pepper

Place the ribs in a roaster pan, cover with aluminum foil, and precook at 300°F for 1 hour.

Remove the ribs from pan and discard drippings.

Separate the ribs and rearrange in the pan.

In a medium bowl, place the catsup, water, vinegar, brown sugar, mustard, paprika, Worcestershire sauce, garlic, chili powder, salt and pepper.

Mix well.

Spoon ½ of the sauce over the ribs.

Bake, uncovered, at 425°F for 10 minutes.

Place pan under the broiler.

Continue to add more sauce until the ribs are evenly coated and well "caramelized."

Serve immediately.

Serves 4–6 people

This basic barbecue sauce is just fine as it is, but you might want to "spice it up" with some of your own favorite flavorings. I add a teaspoon of fresh minced ginger and chill it in a covered jar overnight to let the flavor "mellow".

Pork Roast

7–8   pound boneless rolled pork roast
4   large cloves garlic, cut in half
1   16 ounce can sauerkraut, drained
4   large white onions, quartered
4   large carrots, pared and cut in half
3   cups water

Preheat oven to 375°F.

Make 8 well-spaced stabs in the pork roast with a sharp paring knife.

Insert the garlic clove halves deep into the flesh.

Place in a roasting pan, on a bed of the sauerkraut, surrounded by the onion quarters and carrots.

Add the water and cover with aluminum foil.

Bake at 375°F for 25 minutes per pound, or until a meat thermometer reads an internal temperature of 180°F.

Let roast stand for 10 minutes before slicing and serving.

Serves 10–12 people

They don't get more straightforward than this recipe. Serve this dish with your choice of rice, pasta or potato, and a colorful vegetable.

Spanish Pork Chops

3	tablespoons olive oil
1	medium white onion, diced
6–8	6 ounce pork chops
1	green bell pepper, diced
2	cups diced fresh tomatoes
2	teaspoons salt
2	teaspoons Worcestershire sauce
½	cup water
½	cup uncooked white rice

In a large frying pan, heat the oil over medium-high heat.

Add the onion and cook, stirring often, until lightly browned.

Add the pork chops.

Cook until well browned (about 2–3 minutes per side).

Add the green pepper, tomatoes, salt, Worcestershire sauce and water; mix well.

Sprinkle the rice over the tomatoes and pork chops.

Cover tightly and cook over high heat until steaming.

Reduce heat and simmer for 45 minutes, or until the meat is tender.

Try not to remove the cover — or at least not until the very end.

Serve immediately.

Serves 6–8 people

I wonder why they call them Spanish pork chops. Every ethnic group on the continent makes this recipe. This version is from North Carolina, and I serve it with steamed green beans and carrots.

Upside Down Ham Loaf

★ ★ ★ ★ ★ ★ ★ ★ ★ ★ ★ ★ ★

1   pound ground smoked ham
½   pound lean ground pork
½   pound lean ground veal
2   eggs, slightly beaten
1   cup milk
½   teaspoon salt
¼   teaspoon fresh-ground black pepper
½   teaspoon dry mustard
3   tablespoons minced green bell pepper
1   tablespoon minced onion
4   cups corn flakes, crushed into coarse crumbs
½   cup firmly-packed light brown sugar
1   teaspoon ground cloves

Preheat oven to 375°F.

In a large bowl, combine the meats, eggs, milk, salt, pepper, mustard, green pepper and onion.

Mix well. You'll find using your hands is the easiest.

Add the corn flakes.

Mix thoroughly, again using your hands.

Pat the brown sugar into the bottom of an ungreased 9x13-inch baking pan.

Sprinkle with the ground cloves.

Form the meat mixture into an oblong loaf.

Place in the prepared baking pan.

Bake, uncovered, at 375°F for 1 hour, or until fully cooked.

Let loaf stand for 10 minutes before slicing and serving.

Serves 8–10 people

Purchase a whole smoked ham from the meat counter and ask your butcher to grind it for you. The combination of meats and brown sugar are a delectable variation on an old "standard" of firehouse kitchens.

Cheddary Meatloaf

2   pounds lean ground beef
1   large white onion, diced
2   eggs, slightly beaten
¾   cup salsa
2   cups grated sharp Cheddar cheese
4   tablespoons prepared mustard
¼   cup dill relish
½   cup dry Italian bread crumbs
6   bacon strips, uncooked

Preheat oven to 375°F.

In a large bowl, combine all of the ingredients (except the bacon strips).

Mix well. You'll find using your hands is the easiest.

Form the meat mixture into a large oblong loaf.

Place in an ungreased 9x13-inch baking pan.

Place the strips of bacon across the top of the loaf diagonally.

Cover with aluminum foil.

Bake at 375°F for 45 minutes.

Uncover and continue baking another 15 minutes, or until fully cooked.

Let loaf stand for 10 minutes before slicing and serving.

Serves 8–10 people

This is a classic meatloaf recipe with a twist. The salsa and cheese are delicious! Try adding your own favorite ingredients to the old standard — you may come up with something new!

Beef With Mushrooms

★ ★ ★ ★ ★ ★ ★ ★ ★ ★ ★ ★ ★

1 pound lean round steak
4 tablespoons soy sauce
1 tablespoon cornstarch
1 tablespoon dry red wine
1 teaspoon sugar
4 tablespoons vegetable or olive oil
1½ cups sliced fresh mushrooms
1 small onion, sliced and separated into rings

Slice the steak across the grain into thin strips about ¼-inch wide and 2-inches long. You'll find it easier to thinly slice if it is slightly frozen.

In a large bowl, mix the beef with the soy sauce, corn starch, wine and sugar; set aside.

In a large frying pan, heat 2 tablespoons of the oil over medium-high heat.

Add the mushrooms.

Sauté until the mushrooms become soft (about 2 minutes).

Remove mushrooms from the pan; set aside on a plate.

Heat the remaining oil in the same frying pan, over medium-high heat.

Add the onion slices.

Stir in the beef mixture.

Continue sauteing until the meat is no longer red and the sauce thickens a bit.

Add the cooked mushrooms and mix thoroughly.

Serve immediately over hot rice or egg noodles.

Serves 2–4 people

I always use olive oil if I have it on hand. And I serve this great dish with white or wild rice and steamed carrots.

The Perfect Chili

Seasoning mixture:
- 5 tablespoons chili powder
- 3 tablespoons paprika
- 2 teaspoons cayenne pepper
- 2 teaspoons oregano
- 2 teaspoons garlic powder
- 1 teaspoon ground cumin
- 1 teaspoon fresh-ground black pepper

- 2 pounds ground chuck steak
- 1 pound breakfast sausage, cut into bite-size pieces
- 1 large white onion, diced
- 1 8 ounce can tomato sauce
- 1 8 ounce jar green chili salsa
- 1 4 ounce can green chili peppers, chopped
- 1 16 ounce can tomato paste
- 1 24 ounce can whole tomatoes, chopped, reserve the liquid
- 1 cup beef broth
- 1 16 ounce can pinto beans
- 1 16 ounce can red kidney beans
- 3 12 ounce bottles, or cans, golden beer
- 1 tablespoon hot red pepper sauce
- 2 pounds Cheddar cheese, grated

In a small bowl, combine the seasoning mixture ingredients together and set aside.

In a large saucepan, brown the meats together, over medium-high heat.

Add the onion and ½ the seasoning mixture.

Cook, stirring occasionally, until the onions become soft

Drain excess oil from the pan; set aside.

In a large sauce pan, combine the tomato sauce, salsa, chili peppers, tomato paste, stewed tomatoes, beef stock, pinto and kidney beans, beer and red pepper sauce; mix well.

The Perfect Chili, cont.

Bring to a boil, reduce heat and simmer, stirring often, for 15 minutes.

Stir in the browned meat and the remaining seasoning mixture; simmer, stirring occasionally, for $2\frac{1}{2}$ hours.

Stir in the Cheddar cheese, and continue to simmer for $\frac{1}{2}$ hour more.

Serve hot in warmed bowls.

Makes about 4 quarts

This recipe from the Motor City is "…great after that wintertime stretch" and it's the second version of a timeless classic. This chili recipe is a bit spicier than the Award Winning Homestyle version, and the beer gives it a different flavor all its own. If you're on the job don't worry about using the beer, because the alcohol cooks out and evaporates within minutes of reaching a full boil. Little preparation time and low maintenance are two reasons why this dish is seen so often on the burners of firehouse stoves. Nutrition and ease of service are two others.

Award Winning Homestyle Chili

1	pound mild Italian sausage, cut into bite-size pieces
3	tablespoons olive oil
4	large leeks, diced
2	cups diced celery
4	pounds very lean ground beef
2	tablespoons salt
10	large cloves garlic, minced
3	tablespoons dried cumin
2	28 ounce cans whole tomatoes, chopped, reserve the liquid
¾	cup chili powder
4	tablespoons paprika
4	beef bouillon cubes, crushed
4	chicken bouillon cubes, crushed
1	cup vegetable juice
1	tablespoon dried oregano
1	tablespoon fresh-ground black pepper
3	14 ounce cans red kidney beans, drained
2	large white onions, chopped fine
2	medium green bell peppers, chopped fine

In a large sauce pan, fry the Italian sausage over medium-high heat.

Cook, stirring constantly, until well browned.

Drain on paper towelling and discard all but 2 tablespoons of the oil.

In the sauce pan, combine the olive oil, leeks and celery with the reserved sausage oil over medium-high heat.

Cook, stirring occasionally, until the leeks just become soft.

Add the ground beef, salt, garlic, and cumin.

Cook, stirring often, until the meat is well browned.

Stir in the tomatoes, their juice, chili powder, paprika, crushed beef and chicken bouillon cubes, and vegetable juice.

Award Winning Homestyle Chili, con't.

Reduce heat and simmer, uncovered, for 10 minutes.

Add the sausage meat, oregano, pepper, beans, onion and green pepper.

Simmer for 45 minutes, stirring occasionally.

Cover chili and let stand for 10 minutes before adjusting the spices.

Serve hot with a sprinkle of grated Cheddar cheese or a dollop of sour cream.

Makes about 5 quarts

This is another one of those great recipes that taste better the more they're reheated. Make this in the morning and don't bother to cook again all day.

Shirred Beef And Spinach

1	pound lean sirloin steak
3	tablespoons dry red sherry
2	tablespoons soy sauce
1	teaspoon minced fresh ginger root
1	teaspoon sugar
1	teaspoon oil (sesame is best)
1	14 ounce bag fresh spinach
2	tablespoons vegetable oil
½	cup water
½	teaspoon cornstarch
1	teaspoon chicken base

Cut the meat into thin strips about ¼-inch thick. You'll find it easier to thinly slice the meat if it is slightly frozen for 2–3 hours.

In a large bowl, combine the sherry, soy sauce, ginger root, sugar and oil.

Add the meat and mix well.

Cover and refrigerate for 1 hour, turning the pieces every 10 minutes to coat.

Clean the spinach and cut into bite-size pieces.

In a large frying pan, heat the oil over medium-high heat.

Drain the meat, reserving the marinade.

Add the meat to the hot oil, and brown on all sides (about 3–4 minutes).

Blend the water, cornstarch and chicken base into the reserved marinade; mix well.

Add the marinade mixture to the frying pan.

Cook, stirring often, until it just boils.

Add the cut spinach.

Reduce heat and cook an additional 3–4 minutes, or until the spinach wilts and the sauce thickens a bit.

Serve immediately over hot egg noodles.

Serves 4 people

A member of a Ladies Auxiliary Unit from outside Houston gave me this recipe years ago. She always said she served it often, and it was one of the few ways she could get her boys to eat their spinach.

Beef With Chinese-Style Vegetables

★ ★ ★ ★ ★ ★ ★ ★ ★ ★ ★ ★ ★

1	pound lean round steak, boneless and trimmed
⅔	cup sliced green beans
⅔	cup thinly sliced carrot
⅔	cup thinly sliced turnip
⅔	cup small cauliflower flowerets
⅔	cup thinly sliced Chinese cabbage (Bok-Choy)
2	teaspoons vegetable oil
4	teaspoons cornstarch
½	teaspoon ground ginger
¼	teaspoon garlic powder
1	tablespoon soy sauce
⅔	cup water

Slice the steak across the grain into thin strips about ⅛-inch wide and 3-inches long. You'll find it easier to thinly slice the meat if it is slightly frozen for 2–3 hours

In a medium sauce pan, cover the green beans, carrot, turnip, cauliflower and cabbage with water.

Heat to boiling.

Reduce heat and simmer, covered, for 5 minutes, or until tender but still crisp; drain immediately.

While vegetables are cooking, heat the oil in a wok or large nonstick frying pan over medium-high heat.

Add the beef and stir-fry, turning pieces constantly until the meat is no longer red (about 2–3 minutes).

In a small bowl, mix the cornstarch, ginger, garlic powder, soy sauce and water.

Add the cornstarch mixture to the beef, and heat just until the sauce starts to boil.

Reduce heat and simmer until the sauce thickens slightly.

Serve the hot meat and sauce over the cooked vegetables.

Serves 2–4 people

The taste of the Orient in a recipe from Saskatoon, Saskatchewan! You must serve this dish with white rice.

Lite Beef Stroganoff

¾	pound lean round steak, boneless and trimmed
1	cup sliced fresh mushrooms
½	cup thinly sliced white onion
½	cup beef broth
½	cup water
1	teaspoon catsup
	fresh-ground black pepper, to taste
2	tablespoons all-purpose flour
1	cup buttermilk
2	cups wide egg noodles, cooked and unsalted

Slice steak across the grain into thin strips about ⅛-inch wide and 3-inches long. You'll find it easier to thinly slice the meat if it is slightly frozen.

In a large nonstick frying pan, place the beef strips, mushrooms and onion.

Cook, stirring often, over medium-high heat, until the meat is well browned.

Add the broth, water, catsup and pepper.

Reduce heat, cover and simmer about 45 minutes, stirring occasionally.

In a small bowl, mix the flour with ¼ cup of the buttermilk until smooth.

Add the remaining buttermilk; mix well.

Stir into the hot beef mixture.

Cook, stirring constantly, until thickened.

Serve immediately over the hot egg noodles.

Serves 4 people

A Russian import that's low in calories and high in protein. Serve this recipe with a side of steamed broccoli and yellow squash.

Stuffed Green Bell Peppers

6	large whole green bell peppers, cored and seeded
¼	cup olive oil
1	large white onion, diced
1	large clove garlic, minced
1	pound lean ground beef
2	cups cooked white rice
¼	cup fresh-grated Parmesan cheese
1	tablespoon minced fresh parsley
1	10 ounce can condensed tomato soup
	salt and fresh-ground black pepper, to taste

Preheat oven to 350°F, and lightly grease a 9x13-inch baking pan.

In a large pot of boiling water, blanch the green peppers for 8 minutes; drain well and set aside.

In a large frying pan, heat the oil over medium-high heat.

Add the onion, garlic and ground beef.

Sauté, stirring constantly, until the meat is well browned.

Stir in the rice, Parmesan cheese, parsley and ½ can of the undiluted soup; combine thoroughly.

Season to taste with the salt and pepper.

Using a teaspoon, stuff the peppers with the rice/beef mixture.

Arrange in the prepared baking pan, open ends up.

In a small bowl, combine the remaining ½ can of tomato soup with ¾ cup water; mix well.

Pour over and around the peppers.

Bake, uncovered, at 350°F for 35 minutes, or until the peppers become soft.

Baste occasionally with the pan liquid.

Serve immediately.

Serves 6 people

Lamb Curry

★ ★ ★ ★ ★ ★ ★ ★ ★ ★ ★ ★ ★

2	large green cooking apples
2	tablespoons olive oil
2	medium onions, sliced and separated into rings
1	medium green bell pepper, diced
1	large clove garlic, minced
1	tablespoon curry powder
½	teaspoon salt
½	teaspoon marjoram
½	teaspoon thyme
2	tablespoons all-purpose flour
1	cup canned chicken broth
½	cup dry red wine
1	lemon, juice and grated rind
½	cup dark raisins
2	whole cloves
2	cups diced, cooked lean lamb
¼	cup unsweetened shredded coconut
1	tablespoon sour cream

Core, pare and slice the cooking apples.

In a large frying pan, heat the olive oil over medium-high heat.

Add the onion, pepper, garlic and apples.

Cook, stirring constantly, until the onions become soft.

Sprinkle in the curry powder, salt, marjoram, thyme and flour; mix well.

Cook, stirring constantly, for 5 minutes.

Add the stock, wine, lemon juice and rind, raisins and cloves.

Reduce heat, cover and simmer for 15 minutes.

Add the lamb and coconut.

Mix well, and heat for 15 minutes more.

Before serving, add the sour cream and mix well.

Serve immediately over hot rice.

Serves 4–6 people

This dish, with a taste of the Middle East, is exotic and unusual. Serve it with rice pilaf and sautéed greens.

Famous Fabulous Fowl Fajitas From Joe

4   whole chicken breasts, skinless and boneless
1   cup fresh lemon juice
½   cup Worcestershire sauce
1   tablespoon fresh-ground black pepper
1   teaspoon nutmeg
1   package flour tortilla shells

Slice the chicken into ¾-inch strips.

In a large bowl, combine the lemon juice, Worcestershire sauce, pepper and nutmeg.

Add the chicken strips, turning to coat.

Cover and refrigerate at least 6 hours.

On a preheated barbecue grill, cook the strips, turning often over a high flame, for 10 minutes or until done

Or in a large frying pan, lightly greased with olive oil, sauté the chicken strips, stirring constantly, for 10 minutes or until fully cooked.

Heat the tortilla shells individually in a large nonstick frying pan over medium heat for about 30 seconds per side.

Or heat individually on a plate in the microwave for about 30 seconds.

Serve the hot tortilla shells immediately with a bit of the cooked chicken.

Allow your guests to fill their own fajitas with a bit of the following condiments, set out in individual bowls.

Serve with any or all of these:

diced tomatoes	sour cream
shredded Cheddar cheese	refried beans
diced white onion	sliced black olives
diced jalapeno	guacamole
shredded lettuce	salsa

Serves 8–10 people

Hall #7 Barbecued Orange Chicken

4	large cloves garlic, minced
1	piece fresh ginger root, about the size of a small egg, peeled and minced
1	heaping tablespoon fresh-ground black pepper
½	cup honey
1	12 ounce can orange juice, mixed with 3 cans water
½	cup soy sauce
¼	cup slivered orange peel
2	3–4 pound broiling chickens, quartered
4	tablespoons cornstarch
1	cup cold water

In a very large bowl, mash the garlic and ginger together with a fork.

Add the pepper, honey, reconstituted orange juice, soy sauce and orange peel; mix well.

Add the chicken quarters, turning the pieces to coat well.

Cover tightly with plastic wrap and refrigerate for 24 hours, turning the pieces to coat with the marinade occasionally.

Preheat the barbecue to a medium-low flame.

Arrange the chicken pieces on the grill; reserving the marinade.

Close the lid and barbecue 10–15 minutes per side, or until fully cooked.

In a large sauce pan, heat the reserved marinade to boiling.

In a small bowl, combine the cornstarch and water; mix well and add to the hot marinade.

Reduce heat to a fast simmer, and cook, stirring constantly, for 5 minutes and the sauce thickens.

Serve the barbecued chicken with the marinade in a gravy boat.

Serves 6–8 people

This tasty barbecue dish is juicy, sweet, and spicy. Serve it with a macaroni salad and fresh vegetable for a hearty, filling meal.

Tandoori Chicken

★ ★ ★ ★ ★ ★ ★ ★ ★ ★ ★ ★ ★

8	chicken breast halves, skinned and boned
1	cup low-fat plain yogurt
2	teaspoons crushed coriander seed
¼	teaspoon ground cumin
2	tablespoons minced fresh ginger root
3	large cloves garlic, finely minced
½	teaspoon ground turmeric
½	teaspoon hot red pepper sauce

Trim the fat and tendons from the chicken; rinse and pat dry.

In a large bowl, combine the yogurt, coriander, cumin, ginger root, garlic, turmeric and red pepper sauce.

Mix well.

Add the chicken breasts and turn to coat with the marinade.

Cover and refrigerate for at least 6 hours.

Preheat the barbecue to a medium-low flame.

Arrange the chicken pieces on the grill and barbecue for 8–10 minutes per side, or until fully cooked.

Serve immediately.

Serves 4–6 people

This healthy chicken dish is wonderful with a spicy Greek salad and wild rice pilaf. Don't forget a basket of pita bread.

Chicken Teriyaki And Vegetable Kabobs

2	tablespoons soy sauce
5	tablespoons firmly-packed light brown sugar
2	teaspoons vegetable oil
1	teaspoon ground ginger
⅓	cup dry sherry
½	teaspoon hot red pepper sauce
6	chicken breast halves, skinned and boned
16	fresh mushrooms
2	small zucchini, sliced thick
16	cherry tomatoes
4	medium white onions, cut into 8 wedges each
16	wooden or metal skewers

In a large bowl, combine the soy sauce, brown sugar, vegetable oil, ginger, sherry and red pepper sauce.

Rinse the chicken and pat dry.

Slice lengthwise into ¾-inch wide strips.

Wipe the mushrooms with a clean, damp cloth.

Place the chicken, mushrooms, zucchini, tomatoes and onion in marinade.

Stir to coat evenly.

Cover and refrigerate for at least 2 hours, turning to coat occasionally.

Meanwhile, if using wooden skewers, soak them in water for at least 30 minutes before using to prevent scorching.

Preheat the broiler or barbecue to a medium-high flame.

Remove the chicken and vegetables from marinade.

Alternate the chicken and vegetable pieces on skewers.

On barbecue grill, cook the skewers, for 3 minutes per side or until done.

Or, lay on broiler pan 4-inches away from the heat source. Broil, turning once, for 3 minutes per side or until done.

Serve immediately.

Serves 6–8 people

This nutritious dish is wonderful and should be served with lots of rice.

Rolled Chicken Breasts (Company Chicken)

8	chicken breast halves, skinned and boned
8	slices of bacon
2	8 ounce packages dried beef
2	10 ounce cans cream of mushroom soup
1½	cups sour cream
1	8 ounce can sliced mushrooms, with liquid
¼	cup water
	salt and fresh-ground black pepper, to taste

Preheat oven to 375°F.

Trim the fat and tendons from the chicken; rinse and pat dry.

Fold each chicken breast in half, wrap with a slice of the bacon, and secure with a toothpick.

Rinse and drain the dried beef.

Line the bottom of a 9x13-inch baking pan with the beef slices.

Arrange the rolled chicken breasts on top of the beef.

In a large bowl, combine the soup, sour cream, mushrooms and water.

Mix well.

Pour mixture over the chicken.

Bake, uncovered, at 375°F for 40–50 minutes, or until the chicken is fully cooked.

Season to taste with the salt and pepper.

Serve immediately with egg noodles or wild rice.

Serves 4–6 people

This dish looks a lot fancier and more time consuming than it really is. But no one has to know this…Let it be your secret!

Chicken Marsala

8	chicken breast halves, skinned and boned
3	tablespoons olive oil
4	eggs, well beaten
1	cup all-purpose flour
2	cups chicken broth
2	4 ounce cans mushrooms (pieces and stems)
4	cups Marsala wine
3	tablespoons cornstarch
1	cup cold water

Trim the fat and tendons from the chicken; rinse and pat dry.

In a large frying pan, heat the olive oil over medium heat.

Coat the chicken in the egg, then in the flour.

Arrange in the frying pan, and sauté about 4 minutes per side, or until golden brown.

Remove the chicken from the pan and set aside.

Wipe the oil from the pan with a dry paper towel.

Place the chicken broth, mushrooms and Marsala in the frying pan over medium heat; mix well.

In a small bowl, combine the cornstarch and water; mix well.

Slowly add the cornstarch/water mixture to the hot mushrooms and wine.

Heat to boiling, stirring constantly.

Return the chicken breasts to the pan.

Reduce heat, cover, and simmer for 25 minutes, or until the chicken is fully cooked.

Serve immediately with egg noodles or rice.

Serves 4–6 people

I suggest serving this dish with steamed summer squash or asparagus tips for a fancy meal in under an hour.

Garlic Chicken

★ ★ ★ ★ ★ ★ ★ ★ ★ ★ ★ ★ ★

1   whole baking chicken
1   tablespoon fresh-ground black pepper
⅓   cup olive oil
½   cup all-purpose flour
1½   cups quartered fresh mushrooms
½   cup minced celery
8   large cloves garlic, slivered lengthwise
1   cup red cooking wine

Preheat oven to 350°F.

Remove the skin and portion the chicken into breasts, thighs and drumsticks; rinse and pat dry.

Sprinkle the pepper evenly across the bottom of a 9x13-inch glass baking pan.

In a large bowl, place the flour and chicken and toss to coat all the pieces.

In a large frying pan, heat the oil over medium-high heat.

Place the chicken pieces into the heated oil and fry until well browned (about 2 minutes per side).

Drain the chicken on paper towelling and arrange in the prepared baking pan; set aside.

Add the mushrooms and celery to the remaining oil in frying pan and heat over medium heat.

Sauté until mushrooms just become soft.

Add the garlic and wine.

Heat to boiling, stirring constantly, scraping the bottom of the pan to pick up all the brownings from the chicken.

Pour the mixture evenly over the chicken.

Bake, covered, at 350°F for 45 minutes, or until the chicken is fully cooked.

Serve immediately over brown rice with the pan sauce.

Serves 4–6 people

Broiled Lemon Cajun Chicken

8   chicken breast halves, skinned and boned
1½   cups butter or margarine
3   large cloves garlic, minced
2   tablespoons dried parsley
3   tablespoons cayenne pepper
⅓   cup fresh lemon juice

Preheat the broiler.

Trim the fat and tendons from the chicken, rinse, and pat dry.

In a medium frying pan, melt 2 tablespoons of the butter over medium heat.

Add the garlic and sauté for 1 minute.

Add the remaining butter, parsley and 1 teaspoon of the cayenne pepper.

Simmer for 1 minute.

Spread ½ cup of the butter mixture in a 9x13-inch baking pan.

Arrange the chicken breasts in the baking pan.

Sprinkle evenly with 2 tablespoons of the lemon juice and 1 tablespoon of the cayenne pepper.

Cover the chicken with the remaining butter mixture.

Broil 6-inches from the flame for 10 minutes.

Turn chicken, and sprinkle with the remaining lemon juice and cayenne pepper.

Continue to broil for 10 minutes more, or until the chicken is fully cooked.

Serve immediately with hot rice.

Serves 4–6 people

This dish really goes together fast. I recommend serving it with a bright green vegetable or broiled tomato halves on the side.

Chicken Mostyn

4	chicken breast halves, skinned and boned
1	10 ounce can cream of mushroom soup
¼	cup dry sherry
1	teaspoon garlic salt
1	teaspoon basil
1	teaspoon oregano
½	teaspoon white pepper
1	16 ounce can early peas, drained
1	4 ounce can sliced mushrooms, in liquid

Trim the fat and tendons from the chicken; rinse and pat dry.

In a medium nonstick frying pan, poach the chicken breasts in water for about 10 minutes, or until fully cooked.

Drain and break into large bite-size pieces; set aside.

In a medium sauce pan, combine the soup and sherry over medium heat until smooth (about 2 minutes).

Add the garlic salt, basil, oregano and white pepper.

Bring to a boil, stirring constantly.

Reduce heat and simmer, uncovered, for 15 minutes, stirring often.

Add the chicken pieces, peas and mushrooms.

Continue to simmer 5 minutes more, or until warmed through.

Serve immediately over hot egg noodles or rice.

Serves 4 people

This dish is inexpensive and easy, but it fools lots of people with its blend of "rich" ingredients and hint of sherry.

Southwest Burgers

1 slice whole-wheat bread
1 pound fresh ground turkey
1 egg white
¼ cup finely chopped onion
2 cloves garlic, minced
2 tablespoons minced fresh parsley
½ teaspoon ground cumin
1 teaspoon dried oregano, crumbled
  fresh-ground black pepper, to taste

Make fresh bread crumbs with the bread slice by processing briefly in a food processor, blender, or food chopper.

In a large bowl, combine the bread crumbs, turkey, egg white, onion, garlic, parsley, cumin, oregano and pepper.

Mix well. You'll find using your hands is the easiest.

Cover and refrigerate for 15–20 minutes.

Form into 4 patties.

Preheat the barbecue to a medium flame.

Arrange the patties on the grill and barbecue for 8–10 minutes per side, or until the center is no longer pink.

Serve immediately on grilled hamburger buns, with assorted condiments on the side.

Serves 4 people

An inexpensive and more nutritious variation of an old North American favorite. I like mine on a grilled roll with a dollop of salsa and a paper-thin slice of red onion.

Turkey Divan

★ ★ ★ ★ ★ ★ ★ ★ ★ ★ ★ ★ ★ ★

2	10 ounce packages frozen broccoli flowerets, defrosted
1	pound turkey breast, cooked and sliced thin
4	tablespoons cornstarch
1	cup turkey or chicken broth
1	cup skim milk
⅔	cup grated Cheddar cheese
½	teaspoon salt

Preheat oven to 375°F.

Cook the broccoli according to package instructions, or until just tender; drain well.

Arrange the broccoli in a lightly greased 1½ quart casserole.

Lay the turkey slices on top of the broccoli.

In a small saucepan, mix the cornstarch with broth, over medium heat.

Mix until smooth.

Slowly add the milk.

Cook, stirring constantly, until thickened.

Reduce heat, and add the cheese and salt, stirring constantly, just until cheese melts.

Pour the sauce over the turkey.

Bake, uncovered, at 375°F for 25 minutes, or until the turkey is hot and the sauce is bubbly.

Serves 4–6 people

Don't know what to do with that leftover holiday turkey? This dish makes an easy lunch or dinner served with warm dinner rolls and a crisp garden salad.

Seafood Creole

2   tablespoons butter or margarine
2   tablespoons all-purpose flour
1   10 ounce can whole tomatoes, chopped, reserve the liquid
1   pound large uncooked shrimp, shelled and deveined
1   pound lean fish fillets, cut into large bite-size pieces
1   8 ounce can tomato sauce
½   cup chopped green onions
½   cup diced green bell pepper
⅓   cup minced fresh parsley
2   whole bay leaves
4   large cloves garlic, minced
½   teaspoon salt
½   teaspoon thyme
¼   teaspoon cayenne pepper

In a large frying pan, melt the butter over medium heat.

Blend in the flour, stirring constantly, until the mixture is dark brown — be careful not to scorch.

Pour the reserved tomato liquid into a measuring cup, and add enough water to equal 1 cup.

Slowly stir the tomato liquid into the butter/flour mixture; blend until smooth.

Add the chopped tomatoes, shrimp, fish, tomato sauce, green onion, bell pepper, parsley, bay leaves, garlic, salt, thyme and cayenne pepper.

Mix well.

Simmer, uncovered, for 10 minutes, or until the shrimp and fish are fully cooked; remove the bay leaves.

Serve immediately with cooked rice and lemon wedges.

Serves 6 people

Similar to a shrimp gumbo, only without the okra to thicken the sauce. This recipe comes from Creole country and is a fast way to create one of that region's trademark dishes.

Shrimp Gumbo
(Lonae)

¼	cup olive oil
3	large leeks, chopped fine
1	large white onion, diced
1	cup diced celery
1	pound lean cooked ham, minced
1	pound fresh or frozen okra, chopped
9	large garlic cloves, minced
4	teaspoons ground red chili pepper
1	teaspoon salt
2	teaspoons fresh-ground black pepper
1	28 ounce can whole tomatoes, chopped, reserve the liquid
2	cup vegetable juice
½	cup minced fresh parsley
2	pounds large uncooked shrimp, shelled and deveined

In a large sauce pan, heat the olive oil over medium heat.

Stir in the leeks, onion and celery; sauté just until tender.

Stir in the ham, okra, garlic, chili pepper, salt and black pepper.

Sauté for 15 minutes, stirring often.

Stir in the tomatoes, their juice, vegetable juice and parsley.

Cook, stirring often, over medium heat until the sauce thickens a bit.

Add the shrimp and cook, 7 minutes more, or until the shrimp are fully cooked.

Serve immediately over cooked rice, pasta, or polenta.

Makes about 2 quarts

This decidedly Creole recipe actually comes from a firefighter in Vancouver, B.C. Sometimes referred to as a soup, this hearty dish is really a meal and goes great with a fresh mustard-green salad.

Fisherman's Prize

3	quarts water
18	large uncooked whole shrimp,* shelled and deveined, save the heads and shells
1	quart clam juice
½	cup olive oil
4	leeks, diced small
1	cup diced celery
2	large carrots, diced small
8	large cloves garlic, minced
½	teaspoon thyme
½	teaspoon salt
¼	teaspoon ground red chili pepper
1	tablespoon fresh-ground black pepper
1	28 ounce can whole tomatoes, drained and chopped
2	pounds red snapper or cod fillets, cut into six pieces
¾	cup all-purpose flour
18	mussels, well scrubbed
18	butter clams, well scrubbed

In a large sauce pan, bring the water, shrimp heads and shells to a boil.

Reduce heat and simmer, uncovered, for 45 minutes.

Strain and discard heads and shells.

Return strained stock to pan and add enough clam juice to make 3 quarts of liquid; cover and simmer.

In a large sauce pan, heat ¼ cup of the oil over medium-high heat.

Add the leeks, celery and carrots.

Cook, stirring often, for 10 minutes, or until the vegetables are soft.

Add the garlic, thyme, salt, red and black peppers.

Continue to sauté for another 2 minutes.

Stir in the tomatoes and the shrimp/clam stock.

Reduce heat, cover, and simmer for 15 minutes.

Meanwhile, in a large frying pan, heat the remaining oil over medium-high heat.

Generously dust the cod with the flour.

Fisherman's Prize, con't..

Fry in the hot oil until golden brown and quite firm, about 2 minutes per side; drain well and keep warm.

Place the individual cooked cod pieces into large soup bowls.

Bring the stock mixture to a rapid boil.

Add the shrimp, mussels, and clams.

Cook 7 minutes, or until all the clams and mussels have opened (those that haven't after 8 minutes, discard).

Ladle portions over the fried cod.

Serve immediately with fresh lemon wedges.

Serves 6–8 people

*If whole shrimp can't be found in your area, use uncooked shrimp tails, which are readily available almost everywhere. You'll have to substitute 4 cups of canned fish stock for 1 quart of the water in the very beginning. Clean, devein, and save the shells from the tails and continue as directed.

This meal from the Pacific Northwest is truly a blue ribbon winner! Serve with a side of boiled red potatoes, some green beans, and warm whole grain bread, and enjoy this hearty prize of a meal.

Haz-Mat #12 Shrimp Scampi

2½ pounds large uncooked shrimp, shelled and deveined
1 cup butter
½ cup olive oil
2 tablespoons dried parsley
½ teaspoon thyme
1 tablespoon basil
3 cups sliced mushrooms
7 large cloves garlic, minced
1 cup fresh lemon juice
2 pounds angel hair pasta, uncooked
2 medium heads broccoli, cut into flowerets
 salt and fresh-ground black pepper, to taste

In a large sauce pan, bring 3 quarts of water to a rolling boil.

Add the shrimp, and boil for 3 minutes; drain and set aside.

In a large frying pan, melt the butter over medium heat.

Stir in the olive oil, parsley, thyme, basil, mushrooms and garlic.

Cover and simmer for 10 minutes.

Remove from heat, stir in the lemon juice and set aside.

In a large sauce pan, cook the broccoli in 1½ quarts boiling water for 5 minutes or until tender; drain and set aside.

Cook the angel hair pasta according to package instructions; drain well.

Place the pasta in the bottom of a 9x13-inch baking pan.

Arrange the shrimp and broccoli flowerets over the pasta.

Pour the garlic/mushroom mixture evenly over the shrimp and broccoli.

Place under a preheated broiler for 6 minutes, or until the shrimp are fully cooked.

Season with the salt and pepper; serve immediately.

Serves 8–10 people

This variation of an old restaurant favorite is no "haz-mat" but really a "must-hav-mat." Watch this meal disappear when you serve it with fresh French bread and a salad of mixed greens with a creamy honey dressing.

Golden Fried Shrimp

1½ pounds large uncooked shrimp, shelled and deveined
1 egg yolk
2 egg whites
1 teaspoon salt
¼ cup all-purpose flour
½ cup finely-crushed plain salt crackers
vegetable oil for deep frying

"Butterfly" the shrimp and rinse under cold running water.

In a shallow bowl, combine the eggs and salt; beat well

In another bowl, combine the flour and cracker crumbs.

Dip each shrimp first in the egg mixture, then roll in the cracker mixture; pressing on lightly to coat completely.

Repeat procedure until all shrimp are coated.

In a large deep pot, heat 3-inches of the oil to 365°F.

Deep-fry the shrimp for 2–3 minutes, or until golden brown.

Drain well on paper towelling.

Serve immediately with fresh lemon wedges.

Serves about 6 people

These shrimp, usually served in a basket with a side of cole slaw, also make a tasty appetizer when dipped in a tangy cocktail sauce.

Stone Crab Claws

Stone Crab Claws, about one pound per person
Red Dipping Sauce
Mustard Dipping Sauce

To prepare *raw* claws, place in boiling salted water for 10–15 minutes, or until fully cooked.

To prepare *frozen, cooked* claws, defrost under cold running water or in the refrigerator.

To serve warm; steam the claws for 3 minutes, or until hot being careful not to overcook.

Red Dipping Sauce:
1   cup catsup
3   tablespoons lemon juice
1   tablespoon prepared horseradish
½   teaspoon celery salt
     red hot pepper sauce to taste

In a small bowl, combine all ingredients; mix well.

Makes about 1½ cups

Mustard Dipping Sauce:
¾   cup "lite" mayonnaise or sour cream
¼   cup prepared yellow mustard
2   tablespoons prepared horseradish
2   teaspoons Worcestershire sauce

In a small bowl, combine all ingredients; mix well.

Makes about 1¼ cups

Serve the cooked claws warm or cold with fresh lemon wedges and a side of dipping sauce.

Crack them by holding firmly in one hand, and striking them with a large spoon handle or by using large nut or seafood crackers. Please be careful, the shells can sometimes be as sharp as porcelain.

Enjoy by dipping in a spicy sauce. This delicacy should be served with plenty of napkins. While they require a little "arm work," you'll be rewarded with a sweet, tender, white meat packed with flavor.

Adriatic Prawns

★ ★ ★ ★ ★ ★ ★ ★ ★ ★ ★ ★ ★

30	large uncooked prawns
$\frac{1}{3}$	cup olive oil
$\frac{1}{2}$	cup all-purpose flour
3	large leeks, chopped fine
2	cups fresh parsley, minced
10	large cloves garlic, minced
1	28 ounce can tomato puree
1	tablespoon tomato paste
2	cups clam juice
$1\frac{1}{2}$	cups water
1	tablespoon white vinegar
1	teaspoon salt
1	teaspoon fresh-ground black pepper

With a sharp pair of kitchen scissors cut the legs and snout off the prawns.

Rinse and set aside.

In a large sauce pan, heat the oil over medium-high heat.

Add the flour.

Cook, stirring constantly, until the flour and oil are well combined.

Remove from heat and add the leeks, mixing well to coat.

Return to the stove, reduce heat to low and cook, stirring often, until the leeks become soft (about 5 minutes).

Stir in the parsley and garlic.

Cook, stirring constantly, 1 minute more.

Stir in the tomato puree, the tomato paste, clam juice, water, vinegar, salt and pepper.

Simmer, uncovered, for 30 minutes.

Stir in the prawns and simmer, uncovered, 12–20 minutes more, or until the prawns are fully cooked.

Serve over cooked rice, pasta or polenta.

Serves 8–10 people

This recipe comes from Canada's West coast, where a great variety of seafood is readily available. If prawns aren't available near you, use large fresh whole shrimp, which to everyone but the connoisseur are virtually the same thing.

Shrimp Parmesan

4 pounds large uncooked shrimp, shelled and deveined
¾ pound butter or margarine
1 large white onion, diced
3 large cloves garlic, minced
2 cups grated Mozzarella cheese
⅔ cup grated Parmesan cheese
1 16 ounce jar marinara sauce

Preheat oven to 400°F, and lightly butter a 9x13-inch baking pan.

Arrange the shrimp evenly across the bottom of the baking pan.

Set aside.

In a medium frying pan, melt the butter over medium-high heat.

Add the onion and garlic; sauté until soft.

Pour the mixture evenly over the shrimp.

Sprinkle the Mozzarella, then the Parmesan cheese over the shrimp.

Cover the cheeses and shrimp with the marinara sauce.

Bake, uncovered, at 400°F for 15–20 minutes, or until the shrimp are fully cooked.

Serve immediately.

Serves 8 people

Two Italian favorites, tomatoey shrimp and melted cheese, combine to make a wonderful dish. I recommend you serve this dish with a side of pasta tossed with garlic and olive oil, some green beans, and a crisp salad.

The Only BBQ Salmon

1   3–4 pound salmon fillet, deboned
10   large cloves garlic, minced
1   teaspoon salt
4   tablespoons minced fresh parsley
2   tablespoons minced, sun-dried tomatoes
¼   cup olive oil
4–5 cups cooked long grain and wild rice

With a pair of tweezers and a lot of patience debone the fillet. Or be smart and purchase the fillet, already deboned, from your local fish market.

In a small bowl, mash the garlic, salt, parsley, sun-dried tomatoes and olive oil together with a fork.

Cover and refrigerate overnight.

Using a sharp knife, divide the salmon into thirds, cutting across the grain lengthwise. Cut through the flesh but be careful not to cut the skin.

Spread half of the garlic mixture over the salmon and into the slits.

Preheat the grill to low.

Place salmon directly on the grill, skin side down.

Close the lid and cook for about 10 minutes.

Spread remaining half of the garlic mixture on the salmon.

Close the lid and increase the temperature to medium.

Continue to cook for another 15 minutes, or until the flesh separates easily.

Remove salmon from the grill by inserting two spatulas between the skin and flesh. Lift the flesh, but leave the skin on the grill.

You may not be able to remove the entire fish, which is just fine. Simply "break" the fish into portion sizes and arrange on a platter of long grain and wild rice.

Serve immediately with fresh lemon wedges.

Serves 6–8 people

To clean the skin off the grill, turn the heat up to high and close the lid for 10 minutes. The skin will crisp up and can be easily removed. As the title says, this is the only way to have barbecued salmon.

Salmon Tetrazzini

4	ounces spaghetti, uncooked
3	tablespoons olive or vegetable oil
1/3	cup chopped white onion
1/4	cup all-purpose flour
1 1/4	teaspoons seasoned salt
1/4	teaspoon thyme
	fresh-ground black pepper, to taste
2	cups (1 pint) half and half
1 1/2	tablespoons sherry
2	7 ounce cans pink salmon, drained
1/2	cup sliced black olives
1/4	cup chopped green bell pepper
1/3	cup fresh-grated Parmesan cheese
	paprika
	chopped fresh parsley

Prepare spaghetti according to package instructions.

Preheat oven to 350°F, and butter a shallow 1 1/2 quart casserole.

In a large sauce pan, heat the oil over medium-high heat.

Add the onion and cook for about 5 minutes, or until tender.

Blend in the flour, salt, thyme and pepper.

Cook over low heat until mixture is smooth and bubbly.

Reduce heat, and slowly stir in the half and half.

Cook over low heat, stirring constantly, until thickened and smooth.

Stir in the sherry, spaghetti, salmon, olives and green pepper.

Turn into the prepared casserole.

Sprinkle with the Parmesan cheese.

Bake, uncovered, at 350°F for 20–25 minutes, or until hot and bubbly.

Garnish with a sprinkle of paprika and parsley.

Serve immediately.

Serves 4 people

A German friend from Indiana gave me this very Italian recipe. He serves it with warmed Italian bread and a Caesar salad.

Picante Fillets

★ ★ ★ ★ ★ ★ ★ ★ ★ ★ ★ ★ ★

1½ pounds cod fillets
2 tablespoons vegetable oil
1 16 ounce jar mild or medium picante sauce
½ cup Monterey Jack cheese
2 cups cooked white rice

Rinse fillets and cut into serving size portions.

In a large frying pan, heat the oil over medium-high heat.

Add the fish and sear on both sides.

Cover with the picante sauce.

Reduce heat and simmer, uncovered, for 5–7 minutes, or until the fish is fully cooked and flakes easily.

Serve immediately over the hot rice.

Serves about 6 people

If you don't like cleaning lots of pots and pans and want to serve a fast, economical meal, try this recipe. Serve with a steamed vegetable medley and lemon wedges.

Chinese Halibut Broil

1–1½	pounds halibut fillets, skinless
3	tablespoons soy sauce
1	teaspoon salt
½	teaspoon fresh-ground black pepper
½	teaspoon garlic powder
1	tablespoon lemon juice
1	teaspoon onion flakes
1	teaspoon water
	paprika

Preheat the broiler, and lightly butter a shallow 9x13-inch baking pan.

Cut the fish into equal portion sizes.

In a small bowl, combine the soy sauce, salt, pepper, garlic powder, lemon juice, onion flakes and water.

Rub mixture into both sides of the fish.

Place the fish in the prepared baking pan.

Sprinkle with the paprika.

Broil 2-inches from the heat for 6 minutes, or until the fish is fully cooked; turning once.

Serve immediately with fresh lemon wedges.

Serves 2–4 people

A little soy sauce is all it takes to turn a simple broiled fish dish into something with an exotic, Asian flavor. This broiled dish is great served with a stir-fried vegetable medley and white rice.

Stir-Fried Fish

1	pound snapper, drum, or other firm lean fish fillets, skinless
3	tablespoons cornstarch
4	tablespoons vegetable oil
3	tablespoons soy sauce
2	teaspoons white wine
1	tablespoon brown sugar
2	small green onions, chopped
1	cup broccoli flowerets
2	carrots, sliced thin
2	celery stalks, sliced thin
2	tablespoons minced fresh parsley
2	cups cooked white rice

Cut the fish into 1-inch cubes, and coat with 2 tablespoons of the cornstarch.

In a wok or large frying pan, heat 3 tablespoons of the oil over medium-high heat.

Add the fish pieces and sauté until nearly done (about 2 minutes).

Remove fish from the hot oil and drain on paper towelling; set aside.

In a small bowl, combine the remaining cornstarch with the soy sauce, white wine and brown sugar; set aside.

Add the remaining oil to the wok or frying pan and heat over medium-high heat.

Stir-fry the onion, broccoli, carrots and celery until tender-crisp.

Return the fish and add parsley to wok.

Pour the sauce over the fish and vegetables.

Cook until the sauce thickens and the fish is full cooked.

Serve immediately over the hot rice.

Serves 2–4 people

One of the healthiest ways to prepare food is to stir-fry. This dish is wonderful with its dark and glossy gravy.

Swordfish Broil

2	pounds swordfish steaks
2	tablespoons lemon juice
½	cup soy sauce
½	teaspoon ground ginger
1	large clove garlic, minced
1	teaspoon sugar

Rinse the fish and cut into large 1½-inch cubes; place in a large bowl.

In a small bowl, combine all remaining ingredients.

Mix well, and pour over the fish.

Cover and refrigerate 4–6 hours.

Baste occasionally while refrigerating.

Broil fish 4-inches from the heat for 10 minutes, or until the fish is fully cooked and flakes easily.

While broiling, turn the pieces to brown on all sides, and baste with the remaining marinade.

Serve immediately with fresh lemon wedges.

Serves 4–5 people

Meaty, healthy swordfish cubes, with a hint of Asian spices, will surely impress even the most ardent "meat and potatoes" fan. Serve this dish with a side of plain egg noodles tossed with a little butter, salt, and fresh-ground black pepper. And don't forget plenty of fresh lemon wedges.

Fillets in Nut Crust

2 pounds snapper, or other firm lean fish fillets, skinless
⅓ cup all-purpose flour
1 cup fresh whole-wheat bread crumbs
1 cup finely chopped pecans
1 egg yolk
2 egg whites
2 tablespoons olive oil

Cut the fish into serving size portions and lightly dust with the flour.

Combine the crumbs and nuts in a shallow pan.

In a small bowl, beat the egg yolk and whites with 2 tablespoons water.

In a medium nonstick frying pan, heat the oil, over medium-high heat.

Dredge each fish portion, first in the egg wash, then in the crumb-nut mixture, pressing the mixture evenly over the fish to coat well.

Place the fish in the hot oil and sauté on each side for about 2 minutes per side, or until golden brown.

Carefully place the fish on a bake-and-serve platter.

Bake in a preheated 350°F oven for about 5 minutes, or until the fish is fully cooked and flakes easily.

Serve immediately with fresh lemon wedges.

Serves 5–6 people

Enjoy this "fish-fry" variation with a deep-fried flavor and much less fat. This goes great with a side of buttered egg noodles and steamed green beans.

Classic Italian Tomato Sauce

2 tablespoons olive oil
4 large cloves garlic, minced
1 tablespoon basil
½ teaspoon oregano
½ teaspoon nutmeg
1 28 ounce can crushed tomatoes (3½ cups)
1 28 ounce can whole tomatoes, chopped, reserve the liquid
1 28 ounce can tomato puree
2 large carrots, cut into large pieces
   salt and fresh-ground black pepper, to taste

In a large sauce pan, heat the oil over medium-high heat.

Add the garlic, basil, oregano and nutmeg.

Sauté for 1 minute.

Add all the tomatoes, their juice and carrots.

Bring to a boil, stirring constantly.

Reduce heat and simmer, uncovered, for 2 hours, stirring occasionally.

Remove the carrots and season with the salt and pepper.

Serve over your favorite hot cooked pasta.

Makes about 2 quarts

Here's your start. One hour into simmering you can start adding almost anything you have at hand. Just remember that your spaghetti sauce is a tomato-based sauce and should not be a garbage can, so use care not to overdo it. I might add: a fistful of fresh, diced chives, or a pound of well-browned ground beef. A cup of red wine or some sliced mushrooms would also be nice.

Vegetarian Red Sauce

★ ★ ★ ★ ★ ★ ★ ★ ★ ★ ★ ★ ★

⅓	cup olive oil
6	large leeks, minced
3	stalks celery, minced
1	large white onion, minced
15	large cloves garlic, minced
2	large carrots, grated
2	cups fresh parsley, minced
2	teaspoons oregano
1	teaspoon red pepper
1	teaspoon fresh-ground black pepper
4	28 ounce cans whole tomatoes, chopped, reserve the liquid
1	32 ounce container red vegetable juice

In a large sauce pan, heat the oil over medium-high heat.

Add the leeks, celery and onion.

Cook, stirring often, until soft (about 3 minutes).

Add the garlic, carrots and parsley.

Reduce heat to medium and cook for 15 minutes, stirring often.

Stir in the oregano, red and black pepper.

Add the tomatoes and their juice.

Bring to a boil, stirring often.

Reduce heat and simmer, covered, for 30 minutes, stirring often.

Add the vegetable juice and simmer, uncovered, for 1 hour more, stirring occasionally.

Serve over your favorite pasta with fresh-grated Parmesan cheese.

Makes about 3 quarts

This aromatic red sauce is sure to make a vegetarian out of any meat lover—at least on pasta night!

Chili Spaghetti

1	pound ground chuck steak
1	pound lean pork sausage, chopped fine
2	16 ounce jars prepared spaghetti sauce
1	15 ounce can red kidney beans
1	large clove garlic, minced
1	teaspoon chili powder
1	fresh tomato, chopped
1	tablespoon oregano
2	tablespoons hot red pepper sauce
2	teaspoons seasoning salt
¼	cup diced green bell pepper
1	cup sliced mushrooms
¼	cup diced white onion
2	tablespoons fresh-ground black pepper
2	tablespoons sugar
1	pound spaghetti, uncooked, broken into 4-inch pieces

In a large sauce pan, brown the meats over medium-high heat, stirring often.

Stir in the spaghetti sauce, beans, garlic, chili powder, tomato, oregano, red pepper sauce, seasoning salt, bell pepper, mushrooms, onion, black pepper and sugar.

Bring to a boil, stirring constantly.

Reduce heat and simmer, uncovered, for 2 hours, stirring occasionally.

Cook the spaghetti according to the package instructions.

Drain well, and combine with the meat sauce.

Serve hot in warmed bowls with lots of Italian bread.

Serves 10–12 people

Another main dish variation, this one "gets down to business" by combining two great firehouse mainstays: chili and spaghetti. Look in the meat chapter for a more "traditional" chili recipe.

Vegetarian Red Sauce

★ ★ ★ ★ ★ ★ ★ ★ ★ ★ ★ ★

⅓ cup olive oil
6 large leeks, minced
3 stalks celery, minced
1 large white onion, minced
15 large cloves garlic, minced
2 large carrots, grated
2 cups fresh parsley, minced
2 teaspoons oregano
1 teaspoon red pepper
1 teaspoon fresh-ground black pepper
4 28 ounce cans whole tomatoes, chopped, reserve the liquid
1 32 ounce container red vegetable juice

In a large sauce pan, heat the oil over medium-high heat.

Add the leeks, celery and onion.

Cook, stirring often, until soft (about 3 minutes).

Add the garlic, carrots and parsley.

Reduce heat to medium and cook for 15 minutes, stirring often.

Stir in the oregano, red and black pepper.

Add the tomatoes and their juice.

Bring to a boil, stirring often.

Reduce heat and simmer, covered, for 30 minutes, stirring often.

Add the vegetable juice and simmer, uncovered, for 1 hour more, stirring occasionally.

Serve over your favorite pasta with fresh-grated Parmesan cheese.

Makes about 3 quarts

This aromatic red sauce is sure to make a vegetarian out of any meat lover—at least on pasta night!

Fettucini & Tuna Sauce

8 ounces fettucini, uncooked
3 tablespoons butter or margarine
1 cup thinly sliced green onion
1½ cups sliced mushrooms
½ teaspoon salt
1 7 ounce can water-packed tuna, drained
⅓ cup heavy cream
3 tablespoons minced fresh parsley
fresh-grated Romano cheese

Cook the fettucini according to package instructions; drain well and set aside.

In a large frying pan, melt the butter over medium heat.

Add the green onions, mushrooms and salt.

Sauté until the mushrooms give off liquid (about 3 minutes).

Add the drained tuna.

Cook, stirring constantly, for 1 minute.

In a large bowl, combine the cream, parsley and cheese.

Add to the tuna mixture.

Cook, stirring constantly, over medium heat, until the cheese melts and the sauce thickens.

In a large serving bowl, combine the pasta and hot tuna sauce.

Toss until the pasta is well coated.

Serve immediately with a sprinkle of the Romano cheese.

Serves 2–4 people

This quick, stove-top version of tuna noodle casserole is delicious. Compliment it with a fresh green vegetable to round out the meal.

Fettucini Alfredo

¾ cup butter, softened
2 egg yolks
3 large cloves garlic, minced
1 cup cream
1½ cups fresh-grated Parmesan cheese
2 pounds fettucini, uncooked
    fresh-ground black pepper, to taste

In a medium bowl, whip the butter with a wire whisk until light.

Add the egg yolks, one at a time, whipping well after each addition.

Add the minced garlic and whip well.

Gradually add the cream and Parmesan cheese, a bit at a time, until well combined; set aside.

Cook the fettucini according to package instructions; drain well.

Return pasta to the cooking pot.

Pour the sauce over the top.

Heat the mixture, stirring constantly, over very low heat, until just hot and noodles are well coated.

Season with the pepper.

Serve immediately with a sprinkle of Parmesan cheese.

Serves 8–10 people

Italians might serve this dish as a first course, in which case it would serve 12–14 people. However, when you're not serving a large crowd it halves easily.

Hook & Ladder Linguini

8	ounces linguini, uncooked
1	tablespoon butter or margarine
1	cup sliced mushrooms
½	cup sliced celery
2	tablespoons cornstarch
1	cup chicken broth
⅓	cup dry white wine
2	teaspoons lemon juice
¼	teaspoon thyme
	few dashes hot red pepper sauce
½	cup grated Mozzarella cheese
1½	cups cooked chicken, cut into strips
4	ounces fresh spinach, chopped
	fresh-grated Parmesan cheese

Cook the linguini according to package instructions (omitting the salt).

Drain and keep warm.

In a large frying pan, melt the butter over medium heat.

Add the mushrooms and celery; sauté until tender.

Stir in the cornstarch and mix well.

Stir in the chicken broth, white wine, lemon juice, thyme and red pepper sauce.

Cook, stirring constantly, until bubbly.

Reduce heat and add the Mozzarella, stirring constantly just until the cheese melts.

Stir in the chicken and spinach.

Simmer, covered, for 1 minute or until mixture is hot.

Serve immediately over the hot cooked linguini.

Sprinkle with the Parmesan cheese.

Serves 4 people

This pasta dish is perfect after a particularly hard day. It has ingredients from all four food groups and is wonderful with chewy Italian bread.

Vegetable Rotini

1½ cups rotini (corkscrew) pasta, uncooked
1 10 ounce can broccoli & cheese soup
1 3 ounce package cream cheese, softened
¾ cup milk
2 tablespoons Dijon-style mustard
¼ teaspoon fresh-ground black pepper
3 cups cooked, chopped fresh vegetables (broccoli,
 cauliflower, carrots, peas, etc.)*
⅓ cup fresh-grated Parmesan cheese

Cook the pasta according to package instructions; drain and set aside.

In a large saucepan, gradually stir the soup and cream cheese together over low heat.

Add the milk, mustard and pepper.

Cook, stirring constantly, until mixture is well combined and heated through.

Add the cooked pasta, vegetables and Parmesan cheese.

Heat, stirring constantly, until mixture is hot.

Serve immediately.

Serves 4 people

*If desired, you can substitute one 16 ounce bag of any frozen vegetable combination, cooked and drained, for the fresh vegetables.

Like the vegetarian firefighter who gave me this recipe, I would have to agree that there is "no substitute for fresh vegetables." But his wife insisted that he submit it with the variation, "for anyone who is sick of cutting up vegetables."

Tomato-Smothered Baked Shells with Three Cheeses

1	cup chopped white onion
1	tablespoon olive oil
1	pound lean ground beef
3	15½ ounce jars (5 cups) meatless spaghetti sauce
2	large cloves garlic, minced
1	teaspoon basil
½	teaspoon fennel
½	teaspoon red pepper
¼	teaspoon fresh-ground black pepper
1	pound small shell pasta, uncooked
2	cups ricotta cheese
1	egg, slightly beaten
2	cups grated Mozzarella cheese
1	cup fresh-grated Parmesan cheese

Preheat oven to 350°F, and lightly grease a 9x13-inch baking pan.

In a large frying pan, sauté the onion in the olive oil, over medium-high heat until tender (about 3 minutes).

Add the ground beef and sauté, breaking up the large pieces with a wooden spoon, until well browned (about 5 minutes).

Stir in the spaghetti sauce, garlic, basil, fennel, red pepper and black pepper.

Bring to a boil.

Reduce heat and simmer, uncovered, for 10–15 minutes.

Meanwhile, cook the pasta shells according to package instructions (omitting the salt).

Drain well and set aside.

In a small bowl, combine the ricotta cheese and egg; mix well and set aside.

Layer ⅓ of the meat mixture in the bottom of the prepared baking pan.

Tomato-Smothered Baked Shells with Three Cheeses, con't

Layer ½ the shells over the meat, then ½ the ricotta mixture, ½ the Mozzarella, and ½ the Parmesan.

Spoon ½ the remaining meat mixture over the cheeses.

Layer the remaining shells, ricotta mixture, and Mozzarella.

Spoon remaining meat mixture evenly over top and sprinkle with remaining Parmesan.

Bake, uncovered, at 350°F for 45 minutes, or until bubbly and lightly browned.

Makes one 9x13-inch casserole; serves 6–8 people

This "lasagna-like" dish is very hearty and very satisfying. If you happen to be making a large pot of sauce, I'd recommend making up this dish at the same time. It's great with homemade sauce. If you wrap it properly, you can freeze it before baking and it'll keep for months. Defrost it and bake, and you'll find that dinner was never ready so fast.

Stuffed Shells Florentine

★ ★ ★ ★ ★ ★ ★ ★ ★ ★ ★ ★ ★

1	29 ounce jar marinara sauce
1	10 ounce package frozen chopped spinach, defrosted
2	pounds (4½ cups) ricotta cheese
1	12 ounce package grated Mozzarella cheese
2	eggs, slightly beaten
2	tablespoons fresh-grated Parmesan cheese
1	12 ounce package jumbo shells, uncooked

Preheat oven to 350°F.

Cook the shells according to package instructions; drain well.

In a large saucepan, heat the marinara sauce over medium heat just until hot.

Spoon 1 cup of the sauce into the bottom of a large baking pan.

Reserve the remaining sauce, keeping it warm.

Cook the spinach according to package instructions; drain very well.

In a large bowl, combine the spinach, ricotta, Mozzarella, eggs and Parmesan cheese; mix well.

Using a teaspoon, fill each shell with the cheese mixture.

Arrange the shells, with the opening down, in the prepared baking pan.

Bake, uncovered, at 350°F for 20–25 minutes, or until hot and bubbly.

Serve immediately with the reserved marinara sauce.

Serves 6 people

Serve this tasty classic with a sprinkle of minced parsley and Parmesan cheese.

Pasta Verde

6	slices bacon
10	ounces spaghetti or other pasta, uncooked
1	10 ounce package frozen chopped spinach, defrosted
2	large cloves garlic, minced
¼	teaspoon fresh-ground black pepper
½	cup small-curd cottage cheese
	fresh-grated Parmesan cheese

In a medium frying pan, cook the bacon until crisp.

Drain, and reserve 2 tablespoons of the drippings.

Crumble the bacon, and set aside.

Cook the pasta according to package instructions; drain well.

Meanwhile in a medium sauce pan, cook the spinach according to package instructions.

Drain and reserve ¾ cup of the liquid.

In a food processor or blender, place the spinach and reserved liquid, reserved bacon drippings, garlic and pepper; cover and blend until smooth.

Add the cottage cheese; cover and blend until smooth.

In a large serving bowl, combine the drained pasta and the spinach mixture.

Toss until the pasta is well coated.

Serve immediately with the bacon and Parmesan cheese.

Serves 4 people

This wonderful dish is quite versatile. I serve it not only as a main dish, but also as an accompaniment for many chicken and lamb dishes.

Fettucini Fernandez

2 medium heads broccoli flowerets
2 cups diced carrot
½ cup butter or margarine
5 pounds lean cooked pork, cut into 1-inch cubes
3 large cloves garlic, minced
1 pound fettucini, uncooked
1 pound spinach fettucini, uncooked
2 cups ricotta cheese
3 cups sour cream
1¼ cups fresh-grated Parmesan cheese
3 egg yolks
   salt and fresh-ground black pepper, to taste

In a large sauce pan, cover the broccoli and carrots in boiling water and cook for 5 minutes, or until tender-crisp; drain well and set aside.

In a large frying pan, melt the butter over medium heat.

Add the pork cubes and garlic.

Cook, stirring occasionally, until well browned.

Remove from the heat and set aside.

Cook both types of the fettucini together and according to package instructions; drain well.

In a large sauce pan, combine the ricotta cheese, sour cream, Parmesan cheese, egg yolks, salt and pepper; mix well.

Add the pork mixture, carrots and broccoli; combine thoroughly.

Add the cooked, drained fettucini.

Toss, over low heat, until the pasta is well coated.
Serve immediately.

Serves 10–12 people

Pour this hearty dish into a large serving bowl with tongs and garnish it with Parmesan cheese. Add a basket of warm fresh Italian bread with whipped butter, and a crisp tossed salad with a vinaigrette dressing and watch it disappear.

Macaroni and Peas

1	tablespoon olive oil
¾	cup finely chopped white onion
¼	teaspoon salt
¼	teaspoon fresh-ground black pepper
1	15 ounce can tomato sauce
2	cups water
1	15 ounce can early peas, reserve the liquid
2	tablespoons sugar
2	cups elbow macaroni, uncooked
	fresh-grated Parmesan cheese

In a medium saucepan, heat the oil over medium heat.

Add the onion, salt and pepper.

Cook, stirring often, until the onions become soft (about 3 minutes).

Add the tomato sauce, water, peas and their juice.

Reduce heat to medium-low.

Simmer, covered, for 10 minutes.

Stir in the sugar and continue to simmer for 10 minutes more.

Cook the macaroni according to package instructions; drain well.

In a large serving bowl, combine the macaroni and the tomato/pea sauce.

Toss until the pasta is well coated.

Serve immediately with a sprinkle of the Parmesan cheese.

You might have to thin the sauce with a little hot water as it sits.

Serves 4 people

This inexpensive dish actually has its roots back in the Depression. Try it the day before pay day.

Chicken Enchilada Casserole

2	cups grated Cheddar cheese
2	cups grated Mozzarella cheese
2	tablespoons olive oil
1	large white onion, diced small
1	4 ounce can green chili peppers, drained, seeded and finely chopped
1	10 ounce can cream of mushroom soup
4	large flour tortillas, each cut into 6 pie shaped wedges
1	cup salsa, medium or hot
4	cups diced, cooked chicken meat

Preheat oven to 325°F, and lightly grease a 9x13-inch baking pan.

In a small bowl, toss the grated cheeses together; set aside.

In a large frying pan, heat the oil over medium heat.

Add the onion and sauté until soft.

Stir in the green chili peppers, soup and ½ the cheese.

Cook, stirring constantly, over medium-low heat until the cheese melts.

Line the bottom of the prepared baking pan with 9 of the tortilla wedges.

Spread evenly with ½ cup of the salsa.

Cover evenly with 2 cups of the chicken, then ½ of the cheese sauce.

Repeat the layers: first the remaining tortilla wedges, then the salsa, chicken and cheese sauce.

Top with the remaining grated cheeses.

Bake, uncovered, at 325°F for 50 minutes, or until hot and bubbly.

Let stand on a wire rack for 10 minutes before serving.

Makes one 9x13-inch casserole; serves 6–8 people

An easy Tex-Mex recipe. I serve this with a warm corn bread and a crisp garden salad.

Easy Mexican Chicken Casserole

1	10 ounce can cream of mushroom soup
1	10 ounce can cream of chicken soup
1	16 ounce bag salted corn chips
1	medium white onion, diced
1	medium green bell pepper, diced
1	tablespoon garlic salt
1	tablespoon chili powder
2	cups grated Cheddar cheese
1	cup chicken broth
1	10 ounce can crushed tomatoes
4	cups cooked chicken, broken into bite-size pieces
½	cup diced jalapeno peppers
1	cup sour cream

Preheat oven to 350°F, and lightly grease a 9x13-inch baking pan.

In a large bowl, mash the two soups together.

Add all the remaining ingredients except the jalapenos and sour cream.

Mix well.

Pour into the prepared baking pan.

Bake, uncovered, at 350°F for 25 minutes, or until hot and bubbly.

Serve immediately with the diced jalapenos and sour cream on the side.

Makes one 9x13-inch casserole; serves 6–8 people

One bowl, one pan, just a little effort, and this meal is on the table. Serve it with a fresh green salad and watch it all disappear. I was surprised at how good this simple recipe is!

Tuna Fish and Potato Chip Casserole

½	pound low-salt potato chips
2	7 ounce cans water-packed tuna fish, drained
1	10 ounce can chicken noodle soup
2	tablespoons butter or margarine
2	tablespoons flour
1½	cups milk
1	teaspoon celery seed
1	teaspoon poultry seasoning
1	teaspoon Worcestershire sauce
½	cup grated Cheddar cheese
1	tablespoon minced fresh parsley
	fresh-ground black pepper to taste

Preheat the oven to 375°F.

Arrange the potato chips in the bottom of a buttered 9x13-inch baking pan.

Sprinkle evenly with the flaked tuna.

Cover evenly with the soup.

In a medium sauce pan, melt the butter over medium heat.

Stir in the flour, and mix well.

Stirring constantly, slowly add the milk, celery seed, poultry seasoning, and Worcestershire sauce.

Continue cooking until the sauce thickens.

Pour evenly over the tuna/potato chip mixture.

Sprinkle evenly with the cheese, parsley and pepper.

Bake, uncovered, at 375°F for 25 minutes, or until hot and bubbly.

Let stand on a wire rack for 15 minutes before serving.

Makes one 9x13-inch casserole; serves 6–8 people

This recipe has its origins back in the 60's, but its renaissance didn't come until the invention of low-salt potato chips. Flaked salmon or cooked chicken may also be used.

Round Steak Casserole

1 tablespoon butter
2 tablespoons olive oil
1 pound lean round steak, trimmed and cut into
   $\frac{1}{4}$-inch strips
3 tablespoons all-purpose flour
1 cup sour cream
1 envelope instant French onion soup mix
$\frac{1}{2}$ cup milk
1 cup chopped fresh mushrooms
$\frac{1}{2}$ cup chopped white onion
$\frac{1}{4}$ cup fresh-grated Parmesan cheese
1 tablespoon minced fresh parsley

Preheat oven to 325°F, and lightly grease a 9x9-inch baking pan.

In a large frying pan, melt the butter and olive oil over medium heat.

Add the meat and sauté until lightly browned.

Add the flour and sour cream.

Cook, stirring constantly, until the mixture just begins to thicken.

Add the onion soup mix, milk, mushrooms, and onion.

Mix well.

Pour into the prepared baking dish.

Sprinkle evenly with the Parmesan cheese and parsley.

Bake, covered, at 325°F for 1 hour, or until hot, thick and bubbly.

Let stand on a wire rack for 5 minutes before serving.

Makes one 9x9-inch casserole; serves 4 people

Similar to a Beef Stroganoff only without all the fuss. Serve this dish with hot egg noodles and an easy tossed salad.

Spinach Quiche

1	8-inch single crust All-Purpose pie shell, prebaked (see page 174)
1	10 ounce package frozen spinach
8	slices bacon, diced
½	cup diced white onion
3	eggs, slightly beaten
1¼	cups milk
¼	teaspoon salt
¼	teaspoon fresh-ground black pepper
½	cup grated Cheddar cheese

Preheat oven to 325°F.

Prepare the pie shell in an 8-inch pie plate and prebake according to the instructions on page 175.

Cook the spinach according to package instructions; drain and let cool.

In a large frying pan, fry the bacon until the fat begins to melt.

Add the onion and continue cooking until the bacon is golden brown.

Drain on paper towels and pat dry to remove excess oil.

Arrange the spinach evenly across the bottom of pie crust.

Sprinkle with the bacon and onion.

In a medium bowl, place the eggs, milk, salt and pepper; beat very well.

Pour mixture evenly over spinach, bacon and onion.

Sprinkle the cheese evenly over the top.

Bake, uncovered, at 325°F for 50 minutes, or until the center is set.

Let stand on a wire rack for 15 minutes before serving.

Makes one 8-inch quiche; serves 4–6 people

Brunch, lunch, or dinner—this classic quiche has been a favorite meal in many houses for a long time. Serve it with a medley of fresh fruit and a warm whole-grain bread for a well-rounded meal.

Brunch Casserole

1   8 ounce can refrigerated ready-to-bake crescent rolls
1   pound mild breakfast sausage, chopped well
1   cup grated Cheddar cheese
1   cup grated Mozzarella cheese
4   eggs, slightly beaten
¾   cup of milk
½   teaspoon fresh-ground black pepper
    salt, to taste

Preheat oven to 425°F.

Unroll the crescent roll dough and completely line the bottom of a buttered 9x13-inch baking pan.

Press perforations with your fingers to seal completely.

In a medium frying pan, crumble the sausage, and cook over medium heat until well browned, stirring occasionally.

Drain well on dry paper toweling.

Sprinkle the sausage meat evenly over the crescent roll dough.

Sprinkle the cheeses over the sausage.

In a medium bowl, beat together the eggs, milk, pepper and salt.

Pour mixture over the sausage and cheese.

Bake, uncovered, at 425°F for 15 minutes, or until the egg is set.

Let stand on a wire rack for 10 minutes before serving.

Makes a 9x13-inch casserole; serves 8–10 people

I first had this easy casserole at a brunch I attended many years ago outside Cleveland, Ohio. It goes together quickly and cooks just as fast… which makes it perfect for unexpected guests on Sunday mornings.

Lazy Perogy Casserole

★ ★ ★ ★ ★ ★ ★ ★ ★ ★ ★ ★ ★

15	lasagna noodles (1 pound)
2	cups cottage cheese
1	egg, slightly beaten
½	teaspoon onion salt
2	cups mashed potatoes
½	cup grated Cheddar cheese
¼	teaspoon fresh-ground black pepper
½	cup butter or margarine
1	cup diced red onion

Preheat oven to 350°F, and lightly butter a 9x13-inch pan.

Cook the lasagna noodles according to package instructions; drain well.

Line the bottom of the prepared baking pan with 5 of the noodles.

In a medium bowl, combine the cottage cheese, egg and ¼ teaspoon of the onion salt.

Spread mixture evenly over the noodles.

Layer 5 more of the noodles over the cottage cheese mixture.

In a medium bowl, combine the mashed potatoes, Cheddar cheese and pepper with the remaining ¼ teaspoon onion salt; mix well.

Spread mixture evenly over the noodles.

Layer the last 5 noodles on top of the mashed potato mixture.

In a medium frying pan, melt the butter over low heat.

Add the red onion and cook until the onions are just soft.

Pour evenly over the last layer of noodles.

Bake, covered, at 350°F for 30 minutes, or until hot throughout.

Let stand on a wire rack for 10 minutes before serving.

Serve with sour cream.

Makes one 9x13-inch casserole; serves 6–8 people

This casserole is nearly all white and should be served with colorful and crispy vegetables to make it as appealing to the eyes as it is to the taste buds.

Macaroni and Cheese

★ ★ ★ ★ ★ ★ ★ ★ ★ ★ ★ ★ ★

1½ cups uncooked elbow macaroni
1½ cups diced Cheddar cheese
2   tablespoons butter or margarine, melted
2   cups milk
    salt and fresh-ground black pepper, to taste
¼   cup buttered bread crumbs

Preheat oven to 350°F, and lightly grease a 9x13-inch baking pan.

Cook the macaroni according to package instructions; drain well.

In a large bowl, combine the cooked macaroni with the cheese, butter, milk, salt and pepper; mix well.

Pour into the prepared baking pan.

Top with the buttered crumbs.

Bake, uncovered, at 350°F for 45 minutes, or until hot and bubbly.

Let stand on a wire rack for 10 minutes before serving.

Makes one 9x13-inch casserole; serves 4–6 people

Classic firehouse fare. This meal has graced Canadian and American tables for generations. Balance it with a steamed vegetable of your choice and a fresh fruit dessert.

Super Bean Casserole

1	pound lean ground beef
1	tablespoon vegetable oil
1	large white onion, diced
1	large green bell pepper, diced
1	15 ounce can green lima beans, drained
1	15 ounce can red kidney beans, drained
1	15 ounce can pork and beans
½	cup firmly-packed light brown sugar
1	teaspoon mustard powder
½	cup catsup
¼	cup white vinegar
	salt and fresh-ground black pepper, to taste
4	slices bacon

Preheat oven to 350°F, and lightly grease a 9x13-inch baking pan.

In a large frying pan, brown the ground beef in the vegetable oil over medium-high heat.

Add the onion and green pepper.

Sauté until soft.

In a large bowl, combine all the remaining ingredients (except the bacon) with the browned meat mixture; mix well.

Pour the mixture into the prepared baking pan.

Place the bacon strips across the top.

Bake, uncovered, at 350°F for 45 minutes, or until hot and bubbly.

Let stand on a wire rack for 10 minutes before serving.

Makes one 9x13-inch casserole; serves 6–8 people

This one dish meal is hearty and filling, so it'll serve more people than you might think. Try a sprinkle of grated Cheddar cheese and maybe some chives on top.

Eggplant Casserole

3   cups eggplant, peeled and cubed
18 saltine crackers, crumbled
½   cup celery, diced
1   cup sharp cheddar cheese, grated
3   tablespoons blue cheese, crumbled
2   tablespoons pimento, chopped
1   tablespoon butter, melted
½   cup evaporated milk, or cream
salt and fresh ground black pepper, to taste

Preheat oven to 350°F, and butter a 9x13-inch baking pan.

In a large sauce pan, boil the eggplant in 2 quarts of boiling salted water for about 8 minutes or until just tender.

Drain well.

In a large bowl combine the crackers, celery, ½ cup Cheddar cheese, blue cheese, pimento, butter, and evaporated milk or cream.

Add the drained eggplant and fully combine.

Season with the salt and fresh ground black pepper.

Turn into the prepared baking pan.

Sprinkle evenly with the remaining cheddar cheese.

Bake, uncovered, at 350°F for 45 minutes, or until hot and bubbly.

Makes one 9x13-inch casserole; serves 6–8 people

Asparagus & Shrimp au Gratin

1   pound shrimp, peeled, deveined and cooked
2   pounds asparagus, cut into 2-inch pieces
4   tablespoons butter or margarine
¼   cup thinly sliced green onion
4   tablespoons flour
½   teaspoon salt
    fresh-ground black pepper, to taste
2   cups half and half
¼   cup Swiss cheese, grated
1   tablespoon lemon juice
2   tablespoons parmesan cheese, grated

In large saucepan, cook the asparagus in 2-quarts of boiling salted water for 8-10 minutes or until just tender. Drain well.

In a large sauce pan, melt the butter,over medium-high heat.

Add the green onion and saute until just tender.

Add the flour, salt and fresh-ground black pepper, cook, stirring constantly for 1 minute.

Add the half and half in a slow thin stream, stirring constantly.

Cook, stirring constantly until the sauce thickens. Reduce heat to medium, and simmer for about 1 minute.

Add the Swiss cheese, and ¼-cup parmesan cheese, and stir until fully melted.

Add the lemon juice and shrimp. Toss to completely coat the shrimp with the sauce.

Preheat oven to 400°F, and butter a 9x13-inch baking pan.

Place the asparagus in an even layer across the bottom of the baking pan.

Evenly pour the shrimp and cheese sauce over the asparagus.

Sprinkle evenly with the remaining parmesan cheese.

Bake, uncovered, at 400°F for 15 minutes, or until the cheese is lightly browned.

Serves 6 people

Whenever I cook asparagus, I microwave it on high, with a few tablespoons of water in a large bowl covered in plastic wrap. This steams the aspargus, keeping more nutrients and makes clean up time much easier

FIREFIGHTERS

ON SCENE

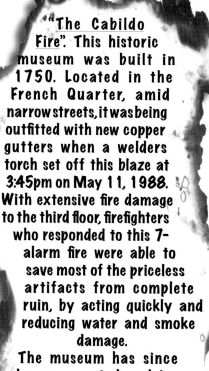

"The Cabildo Fire". This historic museum was built in 1750. Located in the French Quarter, amid narrow streets, it was being outfitted with new copper gutters when a welders torch set off this blaze at 3:45pm on May 11, 1988. With extensive fire damage to the third floor, firefighters who responded to this 7-alarm fire were able to save most of the priceless artifacts from complete ruin, by acting quickly and reducing water and smoke damage.
The museum has since been renovated and is now welcoming visitors.
No injuries were reported.

"Camp Fire Over Lake Ponchartrain" is the call that was heard over the firehouse speaker-phone. In the early evening hours of December 28, 1992, the first New Orleans firefighters on scene were greeted with this inferno.

A total loss, the 1-alarm fire destroyed the approximately 1200 sq. ft. summer home. There were no injuries, and it was brought under control in less than an hour.

PLATE #1 & #2

"Working on the Old Mississip"

On June 20, 1989 this fire at a garage that ware-housed tour trams, repossessed automobiles, and storage facilities was nearly destroyed. The 5:15am call came in from a passing motorist and was responded to by over 100 firefighters, 16 pumpers, and 4 hook and ladders. The 4-alarm fire was just south of Busch Stadium, in downtown St. Louis, home of baseball's Cardinals. The very smoky fire was under control in less than 7 hours, but its timing caused major rush-hour traffic delays. No loss of life was reported, and just one fire-fighter received minor injuries.

"Head Over Heels, and Upside Down in Love with my Job!!!"

These firefighters, with the St. Louis Fire Department, are just two of the 42 member force that comprise the elite, handpicked, Rescue Squad.

They are shown here training with the St. Louis County Police Department, in an exercise designed to coordinate efforts between two different public service departments. These exercises, staged during the day, and at night, are necessary to ensure the safe retrieval of civilians and firefighters from the rooftops of burning high-rise buildings.

PLATE #3 & #4

"Hot Time in Little Havana"

On Valentines Day 1977, this Miami fire in a Little Ha-
vana shopping center, at 12th Avenue and Flagler Street,
burned 12 stores out of business. With as many as
21 units responding to this historic fire, it was finally
brought under control only after 110 firefighters, 16
pumpers, and 5 ladder trucks worked in tandem for
6 hours. The arsonist caused property damage that
exceeded 1 million dollars, and caused 3 firefighters to
sustain minor injuries. Stores and businesses
have since rebuilt.

"Looking into the Mouth of the Beast"

Another arson fire on April 3, 1990, brought Miami firefighters to the scene of this fire, in a vacant warehouse
at N.W. 6th Avenue and 20th Street.
12 units quickly responded to this inferno and property
damage was kept down to $800,000 dollars. Considering
the unusual amount of combustibles present, and the large
open spaces, this fire was still dowsed in under 3 hours.
No injuries were reported.

PLATE #5 & #6

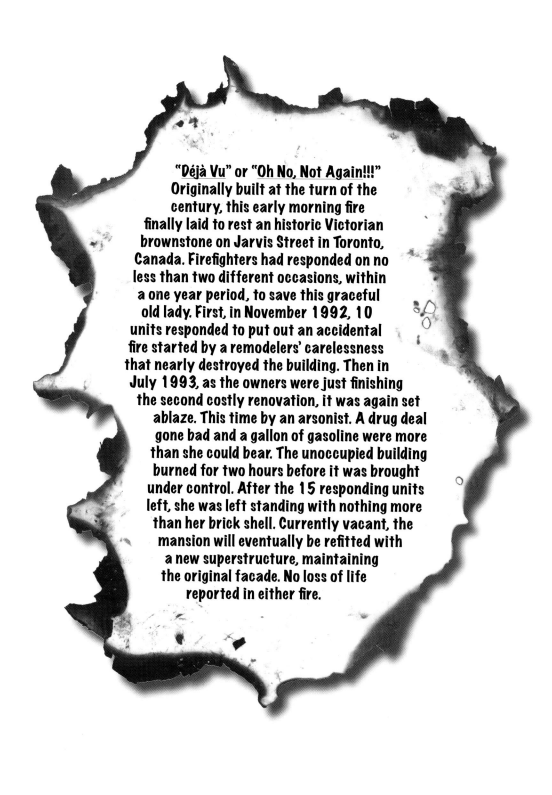

"Déjà Vu" or "Oh No, Not Again!!!"
Originally built at the turn of the
century, this early morning fire
finally laid to rest an historic Victorian
brownstone on Jarvis Street in Toronto,
Canada. Firefighters had responded on no
less than two different occasions, within
a one year period, to save this graceful
old lady. First, in November 1992, 10
units responded to put out an accidental
fire started by a remodelers' carelessness
that nearly destroyed the building. Then in
July 1993, as the owners were just finishing
the second costly renovation, it was again set
ablaze. This time by an arsonist. A drug deal
gone bad and a gallon of gasoline were more
than she could bear. The unoccupied building
burned for two hours before it was brought
under control. After the 15 responding units
left, she was left standing with nothing more
than her brick shell. Currently vacant, the
mansion will eventually be refitted with
a new superstructure, maintaining
the original facade. No loss of life
reported in either fire.

PLATE #7

In Through the Window, Out Through the Door

The Edmonton, Alberta, Fire
Department has been fighting fires
on the edge of the Canadian frontier
since the end of the last century.

The department has 800 firefighters, and
they service a population of approximately
700,000 people, covering an area of about
700 sq. km.

Especially in the winter months, the high winds
and frigid temperatures that are common to the
Canadian plains, often make their job particularly difficult.

The department has grown, and now boasts
a world-class training facility that is used by
firefighters from across Canada.

This photograph, of a fire in a large electrical
supply store, was accidentally started in the
basement. Located in downtown Edmonton, the
fire caused traffic and pedestrian delays on a cold
mid-afternoon in March, 1987.

Station #2 was the first on scene at this
two-alarm fire. Forty responding firefighters
brought it under control in two hours, and in
another two hours, it was completely extin-
guished.

To prevent a backdraft situation, and vent
the fire, firefighters broke through the front
plate glass windows. Realizing the showroom
floors were unstable, these same openings
proved the best avenue of attack.

Although the building was declared a
total loss, no injuries, civilian or
firefighter, were reported.

PLATE #8

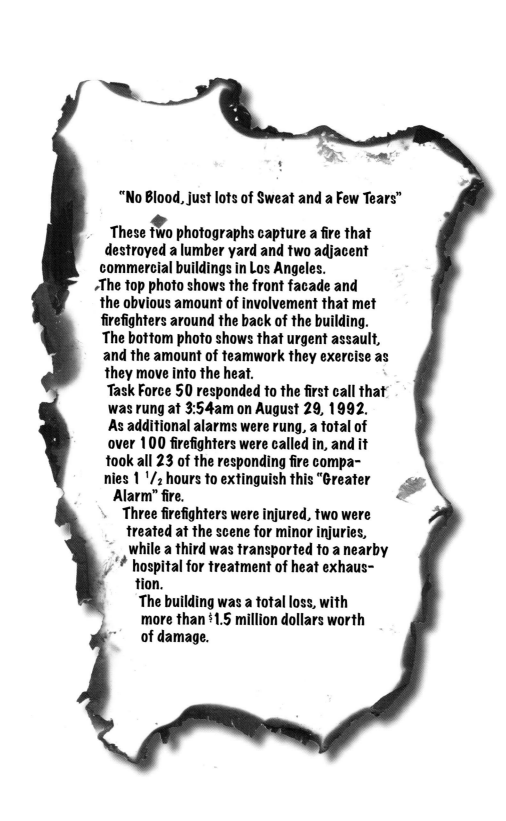

"No Blood, just lots of Sweat and a Few Tears"

These two photographs capture a fire that destroyed a lumber yard and two adjacent commercial buildings in Los Angeles.
The top photo shows the front facade and the obvious amount of involvement that met firefighters around the back of the building. The bottom photo shows that urgent assault, and the amount of teamwork they exercise as they move into the heat.
Task Force 50 responded to the first call that was rung at 3:54am on August 29, 1992. As additional alarms were rung, a total of over 100 firefighters were called in, and it took all 23 of the responding fire companies 1 $1/2$ hours to extinguish this "Greater Alarm" fire.
Three firefighters were injured, two were treated at the scene for minor injuries, while a third was transported to a nearby hospital for treatment of heat exhaustion.
The building was a total loss, with more than $1.5 million dollars worth of damage.

PLATE #9 & #10

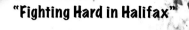

"Fighting Hard in Halifax"

The Halifax, (N.S.) Fire Department
has been fighting fires on the eastern
edge of the continent for over 225 years.
The first record of a firefighting group in the
city dates back to the "Union Fire Club" of 1754,
which was made up of military personnel.
The two photographs submitted to us come from
way back in 1986, and show how even over the
centuries nothing, and everything, changes. Still
putting out fires the old-fashioned way— the
department uses the same determination and
steadfast bravery exercised by generations of their
firefighters. In the upper photograph, on the night of
April 19th 1986, firefighters responded to this blaze
at a fashionable rooming house on Quinpool Road.
A firefighter was injured while saving a man from
the roof. Both men unable to see in the heavy
smoke, lost footing, and fell to a lower roof where
they were rescued by fellow firefighters. The lower
photograph shows the H.F.D. battling a blaze at the
Halliday Craftsman warehouse on Kempt Road.
This fire was fought under intense conditions of
cold and shifting high winds on December 18th,
1986. These wind shifts caused the fire to spread
to an automobile dealership where it blew out of
control for several hours. Damages to the
businesses were total, and caused mil-
lions of dollars worth of loss in stock
and inventory. Five firefighters were
injured, and six department vehicles
were damaged extensively by the
tremendous heat and flames.

PLATE #11 & #12

"Rural Housing and Property Management Technics" This photo shows some clever property management technics from a small community in Oklahoma. The use of training fires is nothing new, but the ability to let them become so involved, without fear of igniting another structure, is rather unique to rural communities. The Edmond Oklahoma Fire Department has Eighty-two full-time firefighters, dispersed amongst 3 station houses, servicing a population of over 50,000 residents, over an area of approximately 100 square miles. Always keeping them in fighting shape, these training fires allow the firefighters to answer the calls quickly and effectively. This process of property management is very effective for the City of Edmond as well. In addition to trying out new firefighting technics, and reestablishing old ones, two other obvious benefits are reducing demolition costs, and helping remove liability from a public hazard.

PLATE #13

STATELY SIDE DISHES

★ ★ ★ ★ ★ ★ ★ ★ ★ ★ ★ ★ ★ ★

★ ★ ★ ★ ★ ★ ★ ★ ★ ★ ★ ★ ★ ★

Stately Side Dishes

★ ★ ★ ★ ★ ★ ★ ★ ★ ★ ★ ★ ★

As the name implies, these dishes are served on the side— and for color, texture and balanced nutrition, we must never underestimate their importance in supporting and complementing the entree.

These recipes include not only fresh vegetables, but also beans, potatoes and rice. You'll find more casserole dishes in this chapter as well, because these seem to work better as the accompaniment than as the main course.

While I'm sure I will hear from those that disagree, there is no "special secret" to cooking vegetables properly. I recommend, and use, the proven and the time honored rules: I take my time, am attentive, don't overcook, and season carefully.

For simple variety, try a squeeze of fresh lemon juice with your greens and carrots, or some fresh-grated Parmesan cheese on your rice or beans. I often try some different ways of cutting and chopping my vegetables. That way, I'm sure not to bore my guests, or myself. A simple example might be to julienne carrots, or cut them on the diagonal, instead of slicing into the usual "thin pennies" before cooking.

As a society, we have long been becoming more aware of the healthful benefits attributed to fruits, vegetables and healthy starches. However, we all too often are still guilty of thinking of the accompaniments as an afterthought, and forget how important they are to the everyday meal. Using care, and forethought, especially in regard to side dishes, are the hallmarks of any fine cook. The vast choice of ingredients available today makes variety accessible to nearly everyone, and a statement that is anything but dull.

Cheese-Fried
Green Tomatoes

½   cup yellow cornmeal
½   cup finely grated Swiss cheese
½   teaspoon salt
¼   teaspoon fresh-ground black pepper
½   cup all-purpose flour
2   eggs, slightly beaten
3   large green tomatoes, cored and cut into ¼-inch thick slices
4–6 tablespoons vegetable oil

In a shallow dish, combine the cornmeal, cheese, salt and pepper.

Place the flour on waxed paper.

In a second shallow dish, beat the eggs slightly.

Dredge the tomato slices in the flour, shaking off any excess.

Dip them in the beaten egg, then in the cornmeal mixture, lightly pressing the mixture onto both sides.

Place on a wire rack.

In a large frying pan, heat 3 tablespoons of the oil over medium-high heat until very hot; but not smoking.

Add one layer of the tomato slices to the frying pan; without overcrowding.

Fry on both sides until crisp and golden (about 2 minutes per side).

Drain on paper towelling.

Sprinkle with salt and keep warm.

Fry the remaining slices, adding more oil as needed.

Serve immediately.

Serves 4–6 people

Finally, a recipe for all those green tomatoes still on the vine just before the first frost!

Herbed Kale

1 quart water
2 tablespoons finely chopped onion
½ teaspoon marjoram
½ teaspoon sugar
fresh-ground black pepper, to taste
1 tablespoon vegetable oil
1 tablespoon butter
2 pounds fresh kale, well rinsed and tough stems removed
OR
2 10 ounce packages frozen leaf kale, defrosted and drained

In a large sauce pan, bring the water, onion, marjoram, sugar, black pepper and oil to a boil.

Add the kale.

Reduce heat, cover and simmer for 25–35 minutes, or until the kale is tender.

Drain well, and toss with the butter.

Serve immediately.

Serves 6 people

This simple deep South recipe was eaten in the homes of slaves long before its delicacy was discovered by cooks across the country.

Scalloped Apples and Sweet Potatoes

3 medium sweet potatoes
4 large red cooking apples, unpeeled, cored, and wedged thin
½ cup firmly-packed light brown sugar
½ teaspoon salt
3 tablespoons butter
½ cup fresh orange juice

Preheat oven to 350°F, and lightly grease a 9x13-inch baking pan.

Bake the sweet potatoes until fork-tender (about 25 minutes).

Peel off the skins and cut into ½-inch thick slices.

Place alternate layers of potatoes and apples in the prepared baking pan; sprinkle each layer with a bit of the sugar and salt.

Dot the top layer with the butter.

Pour the orange juice evenly over the top.

Bake, covered, at 350°F for 30–45 minutes, or until the apples become soft.

Serve immediately.

Makes one 9x13-inch casserole; serves 8–10 people

For a more hearty casserole, add one 7 ounce can of luncheon meat or 1 cup of diced cooked ham. Around the holidays, try a sprinkle of ½ cup dark raisins, and/or ½ teaspoon ground cinnamon.

Beets in Sour Cream

1   16 ounce can whole beets, quartered
¼   cup sour cream
1   tablespoon white vinegar
1   teaspoon minced onion
¾   teaspoon sugar
½   teaspoon salt
    dash of cayenne pepper

In a small sauce pan, heat the beets, in their liquid, until warmed through.

Drain and return them to the sauce pan.

In a small bowl, combine the sour cream, vinegar, onion, sugar, salt and cayenne pepper; mix well.

Pour mixture over the beets in the sauce pan.

Heat the mixture slowly, stirring constantly until hot.

Serve immediately.

Serves 2–4 people

If you like beets (and maybe, even if you don't) you'll love this fast and easy dish with a creamy sweet and tart sauce.

Fire Engine Peas
(Peas & Garlic)

3	tablespoons all-purpose flour
¼	cup olive oil
3	medium white onions, chopped fine
10	large cloves garlic, minced
1	cup fresh parsley, minced
2	tablespoons tomato paste
1	two pound bag frozen peas, defrosted and drained
1½	cups hot water
1	tablespoon fresh-ground black pepper

In a large frying pan, combine the flour and oil over medium-high heat.

Cook, stirring constantly, until the mixture turns the color of dark toast.

Reduce heat to medium-low.

Add the onion, garlic and parsley.

Sauté until the onions become soft (about 5 minutes).

Add the tomato paste; mix well.

Gently stir in the peas.

Add the hot water and black pepper.

Increase the heat to medium-high.

Cook, stirring often, until most of the liquid is gone (about 10 minutes).

Serve immediately.

Serves 10–12 people

This is an inexpensive but tasty way to feed many people. Enjoy it at the end of the week with a mild roast meat or poultry dish.

Barbecued Garlic

★ ★ ★ ★ ★ ★ ★ ★ ★ ★ ★ ★ ★

1	full bulb garlic
1/4	teaspoon olive oil
	dash of salt
	dash of paprika

Slice off the top of the garlic bulb to expose all of the clove tops.

Place bulb on a sheet of aluminum foil and drizzle the olive oil into each of the exposed tops.

Sprinkle with a dash of paprika and salt.

Wrap the foil tightly around the bulb.

Place on the barbecue grill at medium heat for 20–25 minutes.

Serves 8–10 people.

An aromatic accompaniment, squeeze clove by clove onto polenta slices or grilled French bread slices.

Easy Baked Stuffed Tomatoes

8	large fresh tomatoes
¾	cup finely chopped fresh mushrooms
1	10 ounce package frozen chopped spinach, defrosted and drained
¼	cup finely chopped green onion
	salt and fresh-ground black pepper to taste
1	cup grated Monterey Jack or mozzarella cheese

Preheat oven to 350°F.

Cut the tops off the tomatoes, and carefully scoop out the inside seeds, pulp and juice with a teaspoon.

In a large bowl, place the tomato seeds, juice and pulp.

Arrange the cored tomatoes in a shallow 9x13-inch baking pan and set aside.

Add the mushrooms, spinach, and onion to the reserved tomato flesh.

Season with the salt and pepper, mix well.

Spoon mixture evenly into the cored tomatoes.

Cover with the grated cheese.

Bake, uncovered, at 350°F for 25 minutes, or until the tomatoes are soft, hot and bubbly.

Serve immediately.

Serves 8 people

You might want to season this dish with a tablespoon of fresh minced basil, parsley, rosemary or oregano when you're mixing the pulp, but it's really not necessary if you use fresh ripe red thick-walled tomatoes. The ones still warm from the vine are best.

Broccoli-Tomato Pie

$2\frac{1}{2}$ cups cooked white rice
2   eggs, slightly beaten
4   teaspoons butter or margarine
1   tablespoon all-purpose flour
1   cup milk
1   10 ounce package frozen broccoli pieces, defrosted and drained
$\frac{3}{4}$ cup grated Swiss cheese
$\frac{1}{2}$ teaspoon salt
$\frac{1}{4}$ teaspoon fresh-ground black pepper
1   medium fresh tomato, cut into $\frac{1}{4}$-inch thick slices
$\frac{1}{4}$ cup fresh-grated Parmesan cheese

Preheat oven to 350°F, and lightly grease a 9-inch pie plate.

In a large bowl, combine the rice and eggs; mix well and set aside.

In a medium sauce pan, melt the butter over medium heat.

Stir in the flour and cook, stirring constantly (about 1 minute).

Slowly stir in the milk until smooth.

Cook, stirring constantly, until thick and bubbly (about 2 minutes).

Remove from the heat and stir in the broccoli, cheese, salt and pepper.

Return the mixture to the stove, and cook to heat through, stirring constantly.

Stir the broccoli mixture into the rice and eggs.

Turn into the prepared pie plate.

Bake, uncovered, at 350°F for 25–30 minutes, or until the center is almost set.

Remove from the oven.

Increase oven temperature to broil.

Arrange the tomato slices around the outer edge of the pie, and sprinkle with the Parmesan cheese.

Broil 5 minutes, or until golden brown.

Let pie stand on a wire rack for 10 minutes before serving.

Serves 6–8 people

Squash-Broccoli Medley

1	teaspoon butter or margarine
½	cup sliced fresh mushrooms
1	cup small fresh broccoli flowerets
1	cup fresh summer squash, sliced thin
1	cup fresh zucchini, sliced thin
¼	teaspoon salt
¼	teaspoon fresh-ground black pepper
½	cup water
¼	teaspoon fresh-grated lemon peel

In a large frying pan, melt the butter over medium heat.

Sautè the mushrooms until soft.

Add the remaining ingredients, except the lemon rind.

Cover and boil gently for about 6–8 minutes, or until the vegetables are tender; drain well.

Gently stir in the lemon peel.

Serve immediately.

Serves 4 people

The unusual combination of vegetables is what makes this dish. They all compliment each other so well, and adding the zesty lemon peel only heightens their flavor.

Baked Broccoli

2	10 ounce packages frozen broccoli, defrosted and drained
2	cups cooked white rice
1	small onion, chopped fine
1	10 ounce can cream of mushroom soup
1	10 ounce can cream of chicken soup
2	cups grated American cheese
	salt and fresh-ground black pepper to taste

Preheat the oven to 350°F, and butter a 9x13-inch baking pan.

Arrange the broccoli in the baking pan.

Evenly sprinkle with the rice and onion.

In a medium bowl, blend the soups, cheese, salt and pepper.

Evenly pour over the rice and onion.

Bake, uncovered, at 350°F for 20–30 minutes, or until bubbly.

Let casserole stand on a wire rack for 10 minutes before serving.

Makes one 9x13-inch casserole; serves 8–10 people

Former President Bush wouldn't have allowed this dish in the White House, but it's perfect for your house, especially when you haven't got a lot of time.

Yellow Squash and Carrot Casserole

3	medium yellow summer squash (about 8-inches each) cut into ½-inch thick slices
1	cup sliced carrots
1	cup chopped onion
⅓	cup chopped celery
¼	cup chopped fresh parsley
5	tablespoons butter or margarine
1	cup sour cream
1¾	cups dry herb-seasoned stuffing mix
¼	teaspoon dried thyme, crumbled
¼	teaspoon salt
	fresh-ground black pepper to taste

Preheat oven to 350°F, and lightly grease a 1½ quart casserole.

In a large sauce pan, cover the squash and carrots in boiling salted water and cook for 8 minutes, or until almost tender; drain well.

In a large frying pan, sauté the onion, celery and parsley in 4 tablespoons of the butter until onion is tender (about 3 minutes); remove from heat.

Stir in the sour cream, 1½ cups of the stuffing mix, thyme, salt and pepper.

Spread ½ of this mixture into the prepared dish.

Arrange the cooked vegetables over the top, reserving ½ cup carrot and 2 cups squash for the top layer.

Spread the remaining sour cream/stuffing mixture over vegetables.

Arrange the remaining carrots and squash across the top.

In a small frying pan melt the remaining tablespoon of butter.

Stir in the remaining ¼ cup of stuffing mix, and toss to coat well.

Sprinkle the buttered stuffing over the casserole.

Bake, covered, at 350°F for 20 minutes.

Uncover and bake 10 minutes more, or until the topping is crisp.

Let casserole stand on a wire rack for 5 minutes before serving.

Makes one 1½ quart casserole; serves 8–10 people

Fried Squash Patties

2 cups coarsely grated yellow summer squash
2 eggs, slightly beaten
2 tablespoons all-purpose flour
1 teaspoon baking powder
   salt and fresh-ground black pepper to taste
1 tablespoon vegetable oil

In a medium bowl, combine the squash, eggs, flour, baking powder, salt and pepper; mix well.

In a medium frying pan, heat the oil over medium-high heat.

Using a ⅓ measuring cup, pour the batter into the hot oil in 3-inch rounds.

Place 4 patties at a time into the hot oil.

Cook, turning once, 3–4 minutes per side or until brown.

Remove from the frying pan and drain on paper towelling.

Sprinkle with salt and keep warm.

Cook, drain and salt the remaining patties.

Serve immediately.

Makes 8–10 3-inch patties; serves 2–4 people

If the summer squash is unusually moist, wrap it in a towel to absorb some of the moisture. Top with cheese slices and fried bacon slices if you choose.

Parslied Mushroom Patties

3 eggs, slightly beaten
3 cups coarsely chopped fresh mushrooms
½ cup all-purpose flour
½ cup seasoned fine dry bread crumbs
⅓ cup finely chopped onion
1 tablespoon dried parsley flakes
¼ teaspoon fresh-ground black pepper
1 tablespoon vegetable oil

In a large mixing bowl, combine the eggs, mushrooms, flour, bread crumbs, onion, parsley and pepper; mix well.

In a medium frying pan, heat the oil over medium-high heat.

Using a ⅓ measuring cup, pour the batter into the hot oil in 3-inch rounds.

Place 4 patties at a time into the hot oil.

Cook, turning once, 3–4 minutes per side or until brown.

Remove from the frying pan and drain on paper towelling.

Sprinkle with salt and keep warm.

Cook, drain and salt the remaining patties.

Serve immediately.

Makes 8–10 3-inch patties; serves 2–4 people

These aromatic patties are perfect as a light lunch served with a drizzle of light cream or cheese sauce and a small tossed salad on the side.

Oven-Fried Eggplant

★ ★ ★ ★ ★ ★ ★ ★ ★ ★ ★ ★ ★

¾ cup seasoned dry bread crumbs
¼ cup fresh-grated Parmesan cheese
1   medium eggplant, peeled and sliced into
    1x1x4-inch "fingers"
⅓ cup olive oil
    salt and fresh-ground black pepper, to taste

Preheat oven to 375°F, and line a baking sheet with foil.

In a medium bowl, combine the bread crumbs and cheese.

In a second bowl, toss the eggplant with the oil.

Roll the oiled eggplant in the crumb mixture.

Place on the prepared baking sheet in a single layer.

Bake at 375°F, for 15 minutes, turning once, or until crisp and golden.

Season to taste with additional cheese, salt and pepper.

Serve immediately.

Serves 2–4 people

Quick Zucchini

½   cup butter or margarine
6–8   small zucchini (about 8-inches each) cut into ½-inch thick slices
3   medium white onions, diced small
4   celery stalks, diced small
3   large cloves garlic, minced
2   16 ounce cans stewed whole tomatoes, drained and chopped
1½ cups grated sharp Cheddar cheese
     salt and fresh-ground black pepper to taste

In a large frying pan, melt the butter over medium heat.

Add the zucchini, onion, celery and garlic.

Sauté until almost tender.

Stir in the stewed tomatoes.

Simmer, stirring occasionally, for 10 minutes.

Remove from the heat and mix in the cheese, salt and pepper.

Serve immediately.

Serves 6–8 people

Just as the title says, this dish is quick, quick, quick! Serve it with any meat or seafood, and if you don't get raves, I'll be disappointed.

Stuffed Zucchini

★ ★ ★ ★ ★ ★ ★ ★ ★ ★ ★ ★ ★

3	medium zucchini (about 12-inches each)
½	cup butter or margarine
3	medium white onions, finely chopped
3	large cloves garlic, minced
3	celery stalks, finely chopped
	salt and fresh-ground black pepper to taste
1	cup dry bread crumbs

Preheat oven to 350°F.

In a large sauce pan, bring 3 quarts of water to a boil.

Add the whole zucchini and cook for 5 minutes.

Drain zucchini, cut in half lengthwise, and carefully scoop out the flesh with a tea-spoon.

In a large frying pan, melt the butter over medium heat.

Add the onions, garlic and celery; sauté until very tender.

Add the zucchini flesh, salt and pepper.

Mix in the bread crumbs.

Scoop the mixture evenly among three of the cored zucchini shells.

Top with the other three halves.

Wrap the zucchini tightly with aluminum foil and place into a dry 9x13-inch baking pan.

Bake at 350°F for 20 minutes, or until hot and tender.

Unwrap, and serve immediately.

Serves 6 people

You can also place the wrapped zucchini directly on a hot grill and barbecue them for about 20 minutes. Make them up early and be ready for dinner effortlessly.

Baked Potato and Zucchini Combo

8   medium baking potatoes, well scrubbed
¼   cup olive oil
1½   cups sliced fresh mushrooms
2   small zucchini (about 8-inches each)
      cut into ½-inch thick slices
1   large red onion, diced small
4   tablespoons minced fresh parsley
½   pound bacon, fried crisp and diced
      salt and fresh-ground black pepper, to taste
1   cup grated Cheddar cheese

Preheat oven to 400°F, and bake the potatoes for 45 minutes, or until a fork pierces the flesh without much resistance.

Cut the potatoes into thick slices and keep warm.

In a large frying pan, heat the olive oil over medium heat.

Add the mushrooms, zucchini, onion and parsley.

Cook, stirring often, until the vegetables are tender.

In a large serving bowl, combine the potatoes, bacon, vegetables, salt and pepper to taste.

Toss until well combined.

Add the grated cheese and toss again.

Serve immediately.

Serves 8–10 people

This is a great way of combining starch and vegetable in one dish. Add a dollop of sour cream and a sprinkle of parsley when you have company.

Scalloped Potatoes

10	medium potatoes, peeled and sliced thin
1	large white onion, finely chopped
6	tablespoons butter or margarine
½	cup all-purpose flour
2½	cups chicken broth
3	tablespoons mayonnaise
¼	teaspoon fresh-ground black pepper
	paprika, to taste

Preheat oven to 350°F, and lightly butter a 9x13-inch baking pan.

Place ½ the potatoes in the prepared baking pan.

Layer the onion and then the remaining potatoes.

In a large frying pan, melt the butter over medium heat.

Add the flour, stirring constantly.

Gradually stir in the chicken broth, mayonnaise and pepper.

Cook, stirring constantly, until the mixture bubbles and thickens.

Pour evenly over the potatoes and onions and sprinkle with paprika.

Bake, uncovered, at 350°F for 1¼ hours, or until the potatoes are tender.

Let pan stand on a wire rack for 10 minutes before serving.

Makes one 9x13-inch casserole; serves 8–10 people

Serve this classic side dish with roast pork or chicken and a crisp salad.

Golden Potato and Cheddar Casserole

6   medium baking potatoes, well scrubbed
2   cups sour cream
⅓   cup diced white onion
1   teaspoon salt
¼   teaspoon fresh-ground black pepper
2   cups grated sharp Cheddar cheese
¼   cup butter or margarine
     paprika, to taste

Preheat oven to 350°F, and lightly grease a 9x13-inch baking pan.

In a large sauce pan, cover the potatoes with water.

Bring to a boil, reduce heat and simmer 25 minutes, or until almost tender.

Drain, cool, skin and coarsely grate the potatoes.

In a large bowl, combine the potatoes, sour cream, onion, salt and pepper; mix well and set aside.

In a small sauce pan, stirring constantly, melt the cheese and butter together, over very low heat.

Remove from the heat.

Pour over the potato mixture and mix well.

Pour into the prepared baking pan.

Sprinkle with paprika.

Bake, uncovered, at 350°F for 45 minutes, or until lightly golden on top.

Serve immediately.

Makes one 9x13-inch casserole; serves 6–8 people

If you like twice-baked potatoes, you'll love this casserole filled with all the "good stuff." Sprinkle a few chopped chives on top and serve it not only as an accompaniment to dinner, but also as a brunch buffet dish.

Twice Baked Potatoes

★ ★ ★ ★ ★ ★ ★ ★ ★ ★ ★ ★ ★

5 medium baking potatoes, well scrubbed
⅓ cup milk
2 tablespoons butter
½ cup sour cream
1¼ cups grated Cheddar cheese
1 tablespoon dried parsley
1 teaspoon garlic powder
    salt and fresh-ground black pepper to taste

Preheat oven to 400°F, and bake the potatoes for 45 minutes, or until a fork pierces the flesh without much resistance.

Let cool and slice in half lengthwise.

Using a teaspoon, gently scoop out the flesh, being careful not to tear the skin.

In a large bowl, mash the potato flesh with the milk and butter, until smooth.

Add the sour cream, Cheddar cheese, parsley, garlic powder, salt and pepper; mix well.

Spoon the mixture evenly into the empty potato shell halves.

Arrange on an ungreased baking sheet.

Bake at 400°F for 20 minutes, or until the tops become golden brown.

Serve immediately.

Serves 8–10 people

This recipe has been finding its way from house to house, region to region, for decades. If you want an elegant touch, pipe the mashed potatoes back into their shells with a pastry bag, and sprinkle with some chopped chives before re-baking.

Jolley's Haz-Mat Baked Beans

5	10 ounce cans pork and beans, drained
1	pound lean breakfast sausage, cut into ½-inch pieces
1	medium green bell pepper, diced small
1	medium red onion, diced small
¼	cup firmly-packed light brown sugar
¼	cup honey
¼	cup Worcestershire sauce
4	tablespoons catsup
4	tablespoons A.1. Steak Sauce
2	tablespoons prepared yellow mustard
½	cup prepared barbecue sauce

Preheat oven to 350°F, and lightly grease a 9x13-inch baking pan.

In a large bowl, combine all the ingredients; mix well.

Pour into the prepared baking pan.

Cover with aluminum foil.

Bake, stirring occasionally, at 350°F for 1 hour, or until hot and some of the liquid is absorbed.

Serve hot or cold.

Serves about 10 people

Baked beans are required fare at any firehouse barbecue from March to September. Easy, nutritious, and filling — no wonder such a no-nonsense dish would be a staple in North America's firehouse kitchens.

Southern-Style Black-Eyed Peas

1	pound dried black-eyed peas
½	medium onion, diced
1	medium carrot, sliced thin
4	ounces smoke-flavored lean ham, visible fat removed and diced small
5	cups water

Rinse peas under cold running water for 10 minutes.

In a large sauce pan or Dutch oven, combine all the ingredients; mix well.

Bring to a boil and skim off any foam.

Add two additional cups of water and reduce heat to medium-low.

Cover and simmer, for 2 hours, stirring often, or until the peas are plump and tender.

Serve hot with a slotted spoon.

Makes about 1½ quarts; serves about 10 people

Crockpot directions: Rinse peas under cold running water. Place all ingredients in crockpot. Cook on low setting 8–10 hours, or until peas are tender.

This Southern classic comes from Alabama. It has a flavor that should be experienced more often in other parts of the United States and Canada.

Herbed Potato Bake

¼ cup butter or margarine, melted
1 teaspoon seasoned salt
½ teaspoon fresh-ground black pepper
¼ teaspoon dried oregano
¼ teaspoon dried thyme
¼ teaspoon dried marjoram
4 large potatoes, sliced thin
2 medium onions, sliced thin and separated into rings

Preheat oven to 350°F, and lightly grease a 9x13-inch baking pan.

In a large bowl, mix the butter, salt, pepper, oregano, thyme and marjoram.

Add the potatoes and onions and toss until well coated.

Turn into the prepared baking pan and cover with aluminum foil.

Bake, uncovered, at 350°F for 1 hour, or until the potatoes are tender.

Serve immediately.

Makes 1 9x13-inch casserole; serves 6–8 people

This easy potato recipe is perfect to accompany an outdoor barbecue. Make it up early in the day and pop it into the oven just before you head out to the grill. Its mild seasonings compliment any barbecued meat, poultry, seafood, or game without overpowering them.

Grilled Polenta

4	cups hot water
2	teaspoons salt
1	cup yellow cornmeal
3	tablespoons butter or margarine
¼	cup fresh parsley, minced
½	cup olive oil

In a large sauce pan, bring the water and salt to a full boil.

Add the cornmeal, stirring constantly.

Cook, still stirring constantly, until it becomes quite thick.

Stir in the butter until melted.

Spread the cornmeal into a 2–3-inch thick circle on waxed paper.

Cover with waxed paper and place in the refrigerator overnight.

In a small bowl, combine the parsley and olive oil.

Slice the cornmeal mixture into 1-inch thick slices.

Place on the barbecue over medium heat.

Brush with the olive oil/parsley mixture.

Barbecue, turning and basting often, for 10 minutes, or until light grill marks appear.

Serve immediately.

Serves 8–10 people

A different kind of side dish, this is easy to make the day ahead and tend to while you're barbecuing.

Perfect Rice

3 tablespoons butter or margarine
½ cup diced white onion
2 cups uncooked, long-grain white rice
¼ teaspoon salt
1 teaspoon hot red pepper sauce
3 cups fresh or canned chicken broth
1 tablespoon minced fresh parsley
1 whole bay leaf
¼ teaspoon dried thyme
2 teaspoons minced fresh basil

In a medium sauce pan, melt 2 tablespoons of the butter over medium-high heat.

Add the onion and sauté until just soft.

Add the rice and stir, just until well coated.

Add the salt and hot red pepper sauce; mix well.

Add the chicken broth, parsley, bay leaf, thyme and basil. Do not stir!

Bring to a full boil.

Reduce heat, and simmer, covered tightly, for 20 minutes, or just until all the liquid is absorbed.

Let the rice stand, uncovered, for 3 minutes before serving.

Add the remaining tablespoon of butter and toss.

Serve immediately.

Makes about 4 cups; or about 8 ½ cup servings

A bit more subtle than, Wild Rice Pilaf with Carrots and Fennel, but just as versatile. Try this on the side with anything stir-fried or barbecued.

Italian Baked Rice

3 cups cooked long-grain white rice
½ cup grated sharp Cheddar cheese
¼ cup chopped black olives
2 cups canned whole tomatoes, drained and coarsely chopped
1 teaspoon salt
¼ teaspoon fresh-ground black pepper
1 cup corn flakes, coarsely crushed
1 tablespoon butter or margarine, melted

Preheat oven to 350°F, and lightly grease a 9x9-inch baking pan.

In a medium bowl, combine the rice, cheese, olives, tomatoes, salt and pepper; mix well.

Pour into the prepared baking pan.

In a small bowl, toss together the corn flakes and melted butter.

Sprinkle evenly over the tomato/rice mixture.

Bake, uncovered, at 350°F for 30 minutes, or until hot and bubbly.

Serve immediately.

Makes one 9x9-inch casserole; or about 10 ½ cup servings

Wild Rice Pilaf with Carrots and Fennel

2	quarts water
10	tablespoons (1¼ sticks) butter or margarine
1½	cups uncooked wild rice
3	tablespoons ground fennel
4	medium carrots, peeled and cut into large "matchsticks"
1	cup chopped onion
1	cup uncooked long-grain white rice
1	teaspoon dried thyme
1	teaspoon dried tarragon
1	teaspoon salt
4	cups beef stock
1	cup dry white wine
	minced fresh parsley to taste

In a large sauce pan, bring the water to a boil.

Add the wild rice and boil 10 minutes; drain well and set aside.

In a heavy Dutch oven, melt the butter over medium heat.

Add the fennel and carrots; cook, stirring often, for about 4 minutes.

Add the onion, cook and stir another 3 minutes.

Add the wild and long-grain white rice.

Stir to coat with the butter.

Mix in the thyme, tarragon and salt.

Add the stock and wine; bring to a boil.

Reduce heat, cover and simmer, stirring occasionally, for 40 minutes, or until the rice is just tender and all the liquid is absorbed.

Let the rice stand, uncovered, for 5 minutes before serving.

Top with the parsley.

Serves 6 people

This spicy, colorful and crunchy rice dish accompanies grilled lamb or fish perfectly.

QUALITY QUICK BREADS

Quality Quick Breads

★ ★ ★ ★ ★ ★ ★ ★ ★ ★ ★ ★ ★

The bread chapter is a short one and I've included some fast and easy quick bread recipes.

You won't find any of the usual yeast breads, and that's because I didn't want to mire the chapter down with recipes not many of us make anymore. However, if you have the opportunity, and the time, you should experience the delight of working with a favorite yeast dough.

Quick breads are versatile components of the meal every cook should be familiar with. Whether you're planning a brunch menu with a hearty coffee cake, a lunch menu with Banana-Nut Bread, or a dinner menu with a basket of fresh, hot biscuits. As a natural source of fiber, quick breads are a required component of the food pyramid, and also add texture and variety to the meal. And whoever heard of eating a creamed chicken dish without fresh, hot, biscuits to help wipe up the plate.

Cranberry Poppy Seed Loaf

2½	cups all-purpose flour
¾	cup white granulated sugar
2	tablespoons poppy seeds
1	tablespoon baking powder
1	cup skim milk
⅓	cup butter or margarine, melted
1	egg, slightly beaten
1	teaspoon vanilla extract
2	teaspoons fresh-grated lemon peel
1	cup fresh or frozen cranberries, chopped

Preheat oven to 350°F, and lightly grease an 8x4-inch loaf pan.

In a large bowl, combine the flour, sugar, poppy seeds and baking powder; mix well.

In a medium bowl, combine the milk, butter, egg, vanilla and lemon peel; mix well.

Make a well in the center of the dry ingredients and pour in the liquids all at once.

Stir just until the flour is moistened; large lumps are okay.

Gently fold in the cranberries.

Spoon into the prepared loaf pan.

Bake at 350°F for 60–70 minutes, or until a toothpick inserted in the center comes out clean.

Cool slightly, in the pan, on a wire rack.

Remove from the pan, and cool completely on a wire rack.

Makes 1 8x4-inch loaf

This holiday loaf also makes a great muffin recipe that can be served with any summertime lunch.

Cheese, Onion, and Poppy Loaf

3 tablespoons poppy seeds
4 cups all-purpose flour
2 tablespoons baking powder
1½ teaspoons salt
1 teaspoon baking soda
2 cups grated sharp Cheddar or Jarlsberg cheese
3 medium green onions, finely chopped
4 eggs
2 cups buttermilk

Preheat oven to 375°F, and lightly grease three 9x5-inch loaf pans.

In a small bowl, pour boiling water over the poppy seeds and let soak until the seeds sink to the bottom (about 10 minutes).

Drain well, and wring the seeds dry in paper towelling.

In a large bowl, combine the flour, baking powder, salt and baking soda; mix well.

Stir in the poppy seeds, cheese and onions.

In a medium bowl, whisk the eggs until frothy.

Add the buttermilk and whisk to blend well.

Make a well in the center of the dry ingredients and pour in the liquids all at once.

Stir just until the flour is moistened; large lumps are okay.

Divide the batter evenly among the prepared loaf pans.

Bake at 375°F for 35–45 minutes, or until a toothpick inserted in the center comes out clean.

Cool slightly, in the pans, on a wire rack.

Remove from the pans, and cool completely on a wire rack.

Makes 3 9x5-inch loafs

This recipe makes three large loaves, and if you can keep your crew away from them long enough, they freeze wonderfully.

Lemony Date-Nut Bread

1 cup chopped baking dates
2 teaspoons fresh-grated lemon peel
3 tablespoons fresh lemon juice
½ cup butter or margarine, softened
¾ cup white granulated sugar
2 large eggs
2 teaspoons baking powder
½ teaspoon salt
2 cups all-purpose flour
⅔ cup milk
1 cup coarsely chopped walnuts

Preheat oven to 325°F, and lightly grease a 9x5-inch loaf pan, line the bottom with waxed paper, and grease the paper.

In a small bowl, combine the dates, lemon peel and lemon juice; set aside.

In a large bowl, cream the butter and sugar together, until light and fluffy.

Beat in the eggs, 1 at a time, until well blended.

Beat in the baking powder and salt.

Alternately, beat the flour and milk into the butter mixture, stir just until blended.

Gently fold in the date mixture and walnuts.

Spoon into the prepared loaf pan.

Bake at 325°F for 1 hour, or until a toothpick inserted in the center comes out clean.

Cool slightly, in the pan, on a wire rack.

Remove from the pan, and cool completely on a wire rack.

Wrap tightly and let stand overnight before slicing.

Makes 1 9x5-inch loaf

This refreshing bread is tasty when slightly toasted and spread with cream cheese. What makes it especially nice is that it can be made ahead for a fancy twist at lunch time.

Honey-Spiced Squash Bread

★ ★ ★ ★ ★ ★ ★ ★ ★ ★ ★ ★

3	cups all-purpose flour
2	teaspoons baking powder
1¼	teaspoons salt
1	teaspoon baking soda
1	teaspoon cinnamon
¼	teaspoon allspice
2	eggs, slightly beaten
1	12 ounce package frozen winter squash, defrosted
1	cup firmly-packed light brown sugar
¼	cup honey
¼	cup vegetable oil
½	cup coarsely chopped pecans

Preheat oven to 350°F, and lightly grease a 9x5-inch loaf pan.

In a large bowl, combine the flour, baking powder, salt, baking soda, cinnamon and allspice; mix well.

In a medium bowl, combine the eggs squash, brown sugar, honey and vegetable oil; mix well.

Make a well in the center of the dry ingredients and pour in the liquids all at once.

Stir just until the flour is moistened; some lumps are okay.

Gently fold in the pecans.

Spoon into the prepared loaf pan.

Bake at 350°F for 1 hour and 10 minutes, or until a toothpick inserted in the center comes out clean.

Cover loosely with foil during the last 10–15 minutes of baking.

Cool slightly, in the pan, on a wire rack.

Remove from the pan, and cool completely on a wire rack.

Makes 1 9x5-inch loaf

Banana Macadamia Nut Bread

2	cups all-purpose flour
¾	cup white granulated sugar
½	cup butter or margarine, softened
2	eggs, slightly beaten
1	teaspoon baking soda
½	teaspoon salt
1	tablespoon fresh-grated orange peel
1	teaspoon vanilla extract
1	cup (2 medium) mashed ripe bananas
¼	cup fresh orange juice
¾	cup sweetened shredded coconut
1	3½ ounce jar (¾ cup) coarsely chopped macadamia nuts *or* walnuts

Preheat oven to 350°F, and lightly grease a 9x5-inch loaf pan.

In a large mixing bowl, combine the flour, sugar, butter, eggs, baking soda, salt, orange peel and vanilla.

Beat at low speed, scraping the bowl, until well mixed (about 2–3 minutes).

Add the bananas and orange juice.

Continue beating, scraping the bowl, until well mixed (about 1 minute).

Stir in the coconut and nuts by hand; the batter will be quite thick.

Spoon into the prepared loaf pan.

Bake at 350°F for 60–65 minutes, or until a toothpick inserted in the center comes out clean.

Cool slightly, in the pan, on a wire rack.

Remove from pan, and cool completely on a wire rack.

Makes 1 9x5-inch loaf

Tropical bananas, macadamia nuts, and coconut give the taste of Hawaii to this moist and delicious quick bread standard.

Zucchini Bread

1	tablespoon butter or margarine
2	cups all-purpose flour
2	teaspoons baking soda
1	teaspoon baking powder
1	teaspoon salt
1	teaspoon cinnamon
1	teaspoon ground cloves
3	eggs
1¼	cups vegetable oil
1½	cups white granulated sugar
1	teaspoon vanilla extract
2	cups grated unpeeled fresh zucchini
1	cup coarsely chopped walnuts

Preheat oven to 350°F, and generously grease a 9x5-inch loaf pan with the butter.

In a large bowl, sift together the flour, baking soda, baking powder, salt, cinnamon and cloves.

In a medium bowl, beat the eggs, oil, sugar and vanilla until light and thick.

Fold in the grated zucchini.

Make a well in the center of the dry ingredients and pour in the liquids all at once.

Stir just until the flour is moistened; some lumps are okay.

Gently fold in the walnuts.

Pour batter into the prepared loaf pan.

Bake at 350°F for 1 hour and 15 minutes, or until a toothpick inserted in the center comes out clean.

Cool slightly, in the pan, on a wire rack.

Remove from pan, and cool completely on a wire rack.

Makes 1 9x5-inch loaf

When you don't know what to do with all that summertime garden zucchini, make up several of these loaves. I freeze them to give away as great gifts all autumn long.

Cowboy Coffee Cake

½   cup milk
1   teaspoon white vinegar
1¼   cups all-purpose flour
1   cup firmly-packed light brown sugar
¼   teaspoon salt
⅓   cup vegetable shortening
1   teaspoon baking powder
¼   teaspoon baking soda
¼   teaspoon cinnamon
¼   teaspoon nutmeg
1   egg, slightly beaten

Preheat oven to 375°F, and lightly grease and flour an 8x8-inch baking pan.

Sour the milk by adding the white vinegar and setting it aside for 5 minutes.

In a large bowl, combine the flour, brown sugar and salt; mix well.

Using your fingertips, two knives, or a pastry blender, cut the shortening into the flour mixture; it should resemble coarse meal or tiny peas.

Measure ¼ cup of this mixture, and set aside.

To the remaining flour mixture, add the baking powder, baking soda, cinnamon and nutmeg.

In a small bowl, combine the egg and sour milk.

Make a well in the center of the dry ingredients and pour in the liquids all at once.

Stir just until well combined; some lumps are okay.

Spoon into the prepared baking pan.

Sprinkle evenly with the reserved crumb mixture.

Bake at 375°F for 25–30 minutes, or until a toothpick inserted in the center comes out clean.

Cool slightly, in the pan, on a wire rack.

Serve warm or at room temperature.

Makes 1 8x8-inch coffee cake

This easy cake is moist and sweet, and is perfect for a late morning coffee break.

Sour Cream Coffee Cake

Topping:
1   cup white granulated sugar
5   tablespoons finely-chopped walnuts
2   tablespoons cinnamon
2   tablespoons sweetened shredded coconut

Cake:
3   cups all-purpose flour
2   teaspoons baking soda
¼   teaspoon salt
1   cup butter, softened
2   cups white granulated sugar
4   eggs
2   cups sour cream
2   teaspoons vanilla extract

For topping:

In a small bowl, thoroughly combine all ingredients and set aside.

For cake:

Preheat oven to 350°F, and butter a 9x13-inch baking pan.

In a medium bowl, sift together the flour, baking soda and salt.

In a large bowl, cream the butter and sugar until light and fluffy.

Beat in the eggs, 1 at a time, then the sour cream and vanilla.

Add the dry ingredients all at once, and stir just until blended.

Spoon into the prepared baking pan.

Sprinkle evenly with the topping.

Swirl knife through the topping and batter.

Bake at 350°F for 45–50 minutes, or until a toothpick inserted in the center comes out clean.

Cool slightly, in the pan, on a wire rack.

Serve warm or at room temperature.

Makes 1 9x13-inch coffee cake
The sour cream makes it very moist, and a bit tart… Delicious!

Oatmeal Coffee Cake

1   cup uncooked rolled oats
1½ cups firmly-packed light brown sugar
1   cup all-purpose flour
1   teaspoon baking soda
1   teaspoon ground cloves
1   teaspoon cinnamon
1   teaspoon salt
1   cup chopped baking dates
1   cup hot water
½   cup butter or margarine, melted
2   eggs, slightly beaten
3   tablespoons confectioners' sugar, sifted

Preheat oven to 350°F, and lightly grease and flour a 9x9-inch baking pan.

In a large bowl, combine the oats, brown sugar, flour, baking soda, cloves, cinnamon, salt and dates; mix well.

In a medium bowl, combine the hot water, butter and eggs; mix well.

Make a well in the center of the dry ingredients and pour in the liquids all at once.

Stir just until the flour is moistened; some lumps are okay.

Spoon into the prepared baking pan.

Bake at 350°F for 45 minutes, or until a toothpick inserted in the center comes out clean.

Cool slightly, in the pan, on a wire rack.

Remove from the pan, and dust with the sifted confectioners' sugar.

Serve warm or at room temperature.

Makes 1 9x9-inch coffee cake

This is a hearty, sweet cake that is wonderful and quite satisfying early in the morning.

Bob's Blueberry Muffins

2 cups all-purpose flour
1¼ cups fresh blueberries
3 teaspoons baking powder
½ teaspoon salt
½ cup white granulated sugar
1 egg, slightly beaten
1 cup milk
¼ cup butter or margarine, melted

Preheat oven to 375°F, and lightly butter 12 muffin tins (or use paper liners).

In a small bowl, combine ¼ cup of the flour with the blueberries; set aside.

In a large bowl, combine the remaining flour, baking powder, salt and sugar; mix well.

In a medium bowl, combine the egg, milk and butter; mix well.

Make a well in the center of the dry ingredients and pour in the liquids all at once.

Stir just until the flour is moistened; large lumps are okay.

Gently fold in the blueberries.

Spoon into the prepared muffin tins, filling each about ⅔ full.

Bake at 375°F for 20–25 minutes, or until a toothpick inserted in the center of one muffin comes out clean.

Cool slightly, in the tins, on a wire rack.

Remove from the tins, and serve warm or at room temperature.

Makes 12 muffins

When blueberries are in season, Donna and I have been known to eat baskets of these beauties. Serve them with whipped butter or whipped honey-butter and an early-summer brunch will be an affair to remember!

French Road's Famous Spiced Pancakes

1½ cups all-purpose flour, sift before measuring
3 tablespoons white granulated sugar
1¾ teaspoons baking powder
1 teaspoon salt
⅛ teaspoon nutmeg
⅛ teaspoon cinnamon
2 eggs, slightly beaten
3 tablespoons butter or margarine, melted
1 cup milk
¼ teaspoon vanilla extract

Resift the flour with the sugar, baking powder, salt, nutmeg and cinnamon into a large bowl.

In a small bowl, combine the eggs, butter, milk and vanilla; mix well.

Make a well in the center of the dry ingredients and pour in the liquids all at once.

Stir just until the flour is moistened; large lumps are okay.

Lightly grease the griddle or a heavy bottomed frying pan.

Heat to about 365°F, or until a few drops of cold water "dance" when sprinkled on the surface.

Using a ¼ measuring cup, pour the batter onto the hot surface in 4-inch rounds.

Griddle the pancakes until the tops bubble and the edges look dry.

Turn once and brown the other side.

Serve hot.

Makes about 12 pancakes

Fifteen years ago, when on an austerity budget, I gobbled piles of these over the course of several months.

Serve them with lots of warm honey or maple syrup.

DECADENT DESSERTS

Decadent Desserts

★ ★ ★ ★ ★ ★ ★ ★ ★ ★ ★ ★ ★

This chapter is the one I looked forward to writing. As an individual with an overdeveloped sweet tooth, I knew it was one that I would particularly enjoy writing.

Most of the recipes are quite simple and easy to make. Some might take a little more time, the anticipation makes them all the more rewarding.

There are three general rules that apply when choosing desserts:

1. If the meal is three or more courses, or is particularly heavy or rich, select a dessert that is light in composition and piquant (sweet/tart) in flavor.

2. If the meal is made up of leftovers or has been "stretched" to accommodate unexpected guests, select a dessert that is substantial, or at least out of the ordinary, and your guests will surely forgive most any indiscretion.

3. If you are entertaining, and are unsure of your dessert-making abilities, don't attempt a recipe that surpasses your knowledge. If you do, you are sure to end up with a lackluster cake, a "runny" pie filling, or an unrisen soufflé.

My repertoire of pies, cakes and cookies far surpass the limitations presented in compressing them into a single chapter. Naturally, because I love desserts so much, I've added some of my own favorite recipes to lend variety and intrigue, while trying to maintain the integrity of the book.

A proper dessert can make any meal an event, whether you're serving the rich Orange Chocolate Silk Pie, some fresh cookies with a bowl of ice cream, or simply a plate of fresh fruit. And don't underestimate the appeal of fresh fruit. After a particularly heavy meal, a platter of juicy, crisp fruit not only compliments the meal, but is also quite refreshing.

All-Purpose Flaky Pastry

★ ★ ★ ★ ★ ★ ★ ★ ★ ★ ★ ★ ★

2   cups sifted all-purpose flour
$\frac{1}{2}$ teaspoon salt
$\frac{1}{2}$ cup vegetable shortening
2   tablespoons unsalted butter, chilled
5–6   tablespoons ice water

In a medium bowl, combine the flour and salt; use a fork to mix well.

Using your fingertips, two knives, or a pastry blender, cut the shortening and butter into the flour/salt mixture.

When combined, it should resemble coarse meal or tiny peas.

Tossing with a fork, gradually add the ice water, 1 tablespoon at a time. Use only enough water to make the dough leave the sides of the bowl clean, and is soft enough to gather into a ball.

Wrap with waxed paper; and refrigerate at least 30 minutes.

Dust a firm large working surface (preferably wood) and a rolling pin with plenty of flour.

Unwrap the refrigerated dough, and cut into two halves.

With floured hands, shape $\frac{1}{2}$ the dough into a ball.

Roll the dough, from the center out, into a large circle $\frac{1}{8}$ of an inch thick, and about 2-inches larger in diameter than the required pie plate.

Use only as much extra flour as necessary to keep the dough from sticking to the work surface or the rolling pin. Try to handle the dough as little as possible, because it can easily become overworked.

Gently press the dough loosely into the pie plate, trying not to stretch it.

Roll the remaining half of the dough in the same manner, to make either a top crust or another single-crusted pie shell.

Always follow the instructions for filling and baking in the recipes that call for un-baked pie shells.

All-Purpose Flaky Pastry cont.

For recipes that require a prebaked pie shell:

Place the rolled dough loosely into the bottom of the pie tin, flute the edge, prick all over with the tines of a fork, and bake in a preheated 425°F oven for 10 minutes, or until just lightly browned. For a fully baked pie shell: bake for 15–20 minutes. If the dough puffs too much during baking; simply press it gently back down with your hand and continue baking.

Makes two 8 or 9-inch single pie crusts or one 8 or 9-inch double crust

*Note: For a more tender pastry, substitute 1 tablespoon lemon juice or white vinegar for 1 tablespoon of the water.

Variations

Egg and Sugar:
(a cookie-like crust)

Add 1 tablespoon sugar to dry ingredients. Place 1 egg, slightly beaten, in a 1 cup glass measuring cup; add enough water to make about 6 tablespoons.

Lemon or Orange:

Add 2 teaspoons grated lemon or orange rind to the dry ingredients. Place 2 tablespoons lemon or orange juice in a 1 cup glass measuring cup; add 4 tablespoons water.

Make any of these recipes ahead and refrigerate them for 3 or 4 days, or freeze for up to 6 months.

Save your scraps, roll them out, sprinkle with cinnamon/sugar and bake on an ungreased cookie sheet at 400°F for 10 minutes, or until puffy and slightly browned.

Everyone I know has their "own" favorite pie crust recipe. Here's mine. I've included it for anyone who has lost theirs, or wants to experiment with a new recipe. Many of the pie recipes refer back to this page, but if you prefer your own, use it. Always stick with what works for you.

Nut and Crumb Crusts

★ ★ ★ ★ ★ ★ ★ ★ ★ ★ ★ ★ ★

Graham-Nut Crumb crust:
¾   cup finely-crushed graham cracker crumbs
      (about 12 2½-inch square crackers)
½   cup finely-ground walnuts, pecans, or almonds
¼   cup white granulated sugar
⅓   cup butter or margarine, melted

In small bowl, combine all ingredients until well blended.

Press firmly and evenly over the bottom and sides of an 8 or 9-inch pie plate.

Chill until firm, about 30 minutes.

Fill according to recipe.

Almond Crust:
1¾ cups finely-ground unblanched almonds (about 2¼ cups whole)
¼   cup white granulated sugar

In a food processor or blender, combine the almonds and sugar to form a paste.

Press firmly and evenly over the bottom and sides of an 8 or 9-inch pie plate.

Bake in a preheated oven at 375°F for 8 minutes, or until lightly browned.

Cool completely on a wire rack.

Fill according to recipe.

Chocolate Wafer Crust:
1½ cups chocolate wafer crumbs (about 8 ounces of cookies)
2   tablespoons white granulated sugar
⅓   cup melted butter or margarine

In a small bowl, combine all ingredients until well blended.

Press firmly and evenly over the bottom and sides of an 8 or 9-inch pie plate.

Chill until firm, about 30 minutes.

Fill according to recipe.

Key Lime Pie

★ ★ ★ ★ ★ ★ ★ ★ ★ ★ ★ ★ ★

Crust:
1½ cups finely-crushed graham cracker crumbs
    (about 24 2½-inch squares)
2   tablespoons white granulated sugar
½   cup butter or margarine, melted
Filling:
4   eggs, separated
1   14 ounce can sweetened condensed milk
½   cup fresh lime juice
1   teaspoon fresh-grated lime peel
    dash salt
¼   teaspoon cream of tartar
½   cup white granulated sugar

Preheat oven to 350°F.

In a small bowl, combine the graham cracker crumbs with the 2 tablespoons sugar.

Add the melted butter, and mix well.

Press mixture over the bottom and sides of a 9-inch pie plate.

Bake at 350°F for 10 minutes; set aside to cool thoroughly.

Meanwhile, in a large bowl, beat the egg yolks and condensed milk until it begins to thicken.

Thoroughly blend in the lime juice and lime peel.

Pour into the cooled crust.

Add a dash of salt to the egg whites and beat with a rotary beater until foamy.

Add the cream of tartar and continue beating until very soft peaks start to form.

Add the ½ cup of sugar, 2 tablespoons at a time, beating constantly; continue beating until stiff peaks form.

Spread meringue over the top of pie to edge of crust.

Bake at 450°F for 5–8 minutes, or until the meringue is browned.

Refrigerate for at least 6 hours before slicing.

Makes one 9-inch pie

A regional dessert, a national delight. If you're lucky enough to have access to real key limes, by all means use them. The authentic limes are delicious but also a bit tarter so use three tablespoons of sugar.

Frozen Mud Pie

★ ★ ★ ★ ★ ★ ★ ★ ★ ★ ★ ★ ★

1   Graham-Nut Crumb Crust (see page 178)
2   pints coffee ice cream
1   pint chocolate ice cream
1   square (1 ounce) semisweet chocolate
    Rich Chocolate Sauce (see page 210)
    whipped topping (optional)

Prepare Graham-Nut Crumb Crust in a 9-inch pie plate.

Chill 30 minutes, or until firm.

Let the ice cream stand at room temperature to soften to spreading consistency; about 5–8 minutes.

Spoon the coffee ice cream into the crust, higher and thicker around the edges, so that there is a large shallow well in the center.

Fill the well with the chocolate ice cream; smooth top.

Cover with plastic wrap.

Freeze until hard, 2–3 hours.*

To serve, remove wrapping and let the pie soften for 5–10 minutes.

Coarsely grate semisweet chocolate over the top.

Serve immediately with Rich Chocolate Sauce and whipped topping.

Promptly freeze your leftovers.

*Note: If you are making the pie more than a day ahead, remove the wrap after the ice cream is hard. Cover it tightly with freezer paper or foil, and return it to the freezer.

Makes one 9-inch pie

This easy-to-make pie is perfect as a summertime late supper dessert.

Orange Chocolate Silk Pie

★ ★ ★ ★ ★ ★ ★ ★ ★ ★ ★ ★ ★

1	Chocolate Wafer Crust (see page 178)
2	1 ounce squares semisweet chocolate
½	cup (1 stick) unsalted butter, softened
¾	cup confectioners' sugar
2	eggs
1	cup heavy cream
4	tablespoons orange-flavored liqueur
	Orange Whipped Topping (see page 209)

Prepare Chocolate Wafer Crust in a 9-inch pie plate.

Chill 30 minutes, or until firm.

Melt the chocolate in a double boiler over medium heat; cool and set aside.

In a large bowl, beat the butter and confectioners' sugar together until light and fluffy.

Blend in the cooled chocolate.

Beat in the eggs, one at a time, beating well after each addition, (about 5 minutes per egg).

In a small bowl, beat the cream into medium-stiff peaks.

Fold the whipped cream and the orange liqueur into the chocolate mixture just until no white streaks remain.

Turn into the chilled pie crust.

Cover with plastic wrap.

Refrigerate for at least 4 hours, or until firm.

Just before serving, prepare a garnish of the Orange Whipped Topping.

Spoon or pipe the whipped topping around the edge of the pie.

With a vegetable peeler, shave some dark chocolate over the whipped cream.

Serve immediately.

Promptly refrigerate your leftovers.

Makes one 9-inch pie

Peaches and Cream Pie

★ ★ ★ ★ ★ ★ ★ ★ ★ ★ ★ ★ ★

1	9-inch single crust All-Purpose pie shell, unbaked (see page 176)
2	16 ounce cans sliced peaches, well drained
1	cup white granulated sugar
¼	cup all-purpose flour
1	cup heavy cream
2	eggs, slightly beaten

Preheat oven to 375°F, and prepare the pie shell in a 9-inch pie plate.

Fill the pie shell with the peaches.

In a medium sauce pan, combine the sugar and flour.

Stir in the cream.

Cook, stirring constantly, over medium heat, until the mixture just simmers; remove from the heat.

In a small bowl, beat the eggs until light yellow in color.

Stir a little of the hot cream mixture into the eggs, then stir the egg mixture into the cream.

Cook, stirring constantly, over medium heat, until the custard thickens, about 5 minutes.

Pour evenly over the peaches in the pie shell.

Bake at 375°F for 45 minutes, or until the custard sets.

Cool on a wire rack for 30 minutes before slicing.

Serve warm or at room temperature.

Promptly refrigerate your leftovers.

Makes one 9 or 10-inch deep-dish pie

Peaches and a smooth creamy custard bake up into a dessert that's the talk of any party.

Classic Banana Cream Pie

1	9-inch single crust All-Purpose pie shell, prebaked (see page 176)
3	tablespoons cornstarch
1⅔	cups water
1	14 ounce can sweetened condensed milk (not evaporated milk)
3	egg yolks, slightly beaten
2	tablespoons butter or margarine
1	teaspoon vanilla extract
3	medium bananas
¼	cup fresh lemon juice
½	cup heavy cream, whipped
2	tablespoons confectioners' sugar

Prepare the pie shell in a 9-inch pie plate and prebake according to the instructions on page 176.

In a large sauce pan, dissolve the cornstarch in the water over medium heat.

Stir in the sweetened condensed milk and egg yolks.

Cook, stirring constantly, until thick and bubbly; remove from the heat.

Stir in the butter and vanilla; cool slightly.

Slice 2 of the bananas; dip in the lemon juice and drain.

Arrange on the bottom of the prepared crust.

Pour the filling over the bananas.

Cover and refrigerate for at least 6 hours or until firm.

Just before serving, in a small bowl, whip the cream and confectioners' sugar together until medium-stiff peaks form.

Spread the whipped cream over the top of pie.

Slice the remaining banana, dip in the lemon juice, drain, and garnish top of pie.

Serve immediately.

Promptly refrigerate your leftovers.

Makes one 9-inch pie

Pumpkin Pie

1   8-inch single crust All-Purpose pie shell, unbaked
     (see page 176)
1½ cups solid-pack pumpkin
1   egg, slightly beaten
½   teaspoon ginger
⅛   teaspoon allspice
⅛   teaspoon ground cloves
½   teaspoon cinnamon
½   cup plus 2 tablespoons white granulated sugar
     or ¾ cup firmly-packed light brown sugar
½   teaspoon salt
1   cup milk
     whipped topping (optional)

Preheat oven to 450°F, and prepare the pie shell in a 9-inch pie plate.

In a large bowl, combine the pumpkin, egg, ginger, allspice, cloves, cinnamon, sugar, salt and milk; mix until smooth.

Pour the mixture into the unbaked pie shell.

Bake at 450°F for 15 minutes.

Reduce heat to 375°F, and continue baking for 25–35 minutes more, or until a knife inserted in the center comes out clean.

Cool completely on a wire rack.

Serve immediately with whipped topping.

Promptly refrigerate your leftovers.

Makes one 8-inch pie

Variation
Squash Pie:
Substitute cooked mashed summer squash for pumpkin.

Whether you celebrate in October or November, we all know Thanksgiving Day would not be complete without this traditional harvest pie.

184

Sweet-Potato Pie

1	9-inch single crust All-Purpose pie shell, unbaked (see page 176)
2	16 ounce cans sweet potatoes in syrup, drained
½	cup milk
¼	cup light molasses
¼	cup firmly-packed light brown sugar
2	tablespoons butter or margarine, melted
2	eggs, slightly beaten
1	teaspoon cinnamon
½	cup heavy cream
2	tablespoons confectioners' sugar

Preheat oven to 375°F, and prepare the pie shell in a 9-inch pie plate with a high fluted edge.

In a large bowl, mash the sweet potatoes until smooth.

Add the milk, molasses, brown sugar, butter, eggs and cinnamon; blend well.

Spoon the sweet-potato mixture into the prepared pie shell.

Bake at 375°F for 45–50 minutes, or until a knife inserted in the center comes out clean.

Cool pie slightly on a wire rack.

Just before serving, in a small bowl, whip the heavy cream and confectioners' sugar together until soft peaks form.

Place a dollop on each slice.

Serve warm or at room temperature.

Promptly refrigerate your leftovers.

Makes one 9-inch pie

Mississippi makes it with molasses and cinnamon — a true Southern tradition.

185

Strawberry-Pineapple Pie

★ ★ ★ ★ ★ ★ ★ ★ ★ ★ ★ ★ ★

1	9-inch two crust All-Purpose pie shell, unbaked (see page 176)
1	8 ounce can crushed pineapple, well drained
½	cup white granulated sugar
¼	cup cornstarch
2	tablespoons lemon juice
2	pints strawberries, rinsed, hulled and sliced, (about 3½ cups)

Preheat oven to 425°F, and prepare the pie shell in a 9-inch pie plate.

In a large bowl, combine the pineapple, sugar, cornstarch and lemon juice.

Gently stir in the strawberries.

Pour into the pie shell; cover with remaining pastry, or cut the pastry into strips and make a lattice design on top of the pie.

Bake at 425°F for 20 minutes.

Reduce heat to 350°F, and continue baking 35 minutes more, or until the crust is golden and the fruit juices bubble.

Cool on a wire rack for 30 minutes before slicing.

Serve warm or at room temperature.

Promptly refrigerate your leftovers.

Makes one 9-inch pie

Strawberries and pineapple combine to make a delicious fruit pie that is tart and sweet with a fine glossy appearance.

Cola Cake

2 cups sifted all-purpose flour
1 teaspoon baking soda
2 cups white granulated sugar
½ cup butter
1½ cups miniature marshmallows
3 tablespoons cocoa powder
1 cup cola
2 eggs
½ cup buttermilk
1 teaspoon vanilla extract
1 cup semisweet chocolate chips
Cola Glaze (page 210)

Preheat oven to 350°F, and lightly grease and flour a 9x13-inch baking pan.

In a large bowl, sift the flour and baking soda.

Stir in the sugar.

In a medium sauce pan, combine the butter, marshmallows, cocoa and cola.

Over medium heat, stirring constantly, melt the marshmallow mixture; do not boil.

Pour over the flour mixture, and beat until well blended.

In a small bowl, beat the eggs until foamy.

Stir the buttermilk and vanilla into the eggs.

Beat the buttermilk mixture into the flour mixture until batter is smooth.

Stir in the chocolate chips.

Spoon into the prepared baking pan.

Bake at 350°F for 50 minutes, or until a toothpick inserted in the center comes out clean.

Spread the hot cake with the Cola Glaze.

Cool completely, in the pan, on a wire rack before cutting.

Makes one 9x13-inch cake

Lemon Nut Cake

★ ★ ★ ★ ★ ★ ★ ★ ★ ★ ★ ★ ★

¾	cup butter, softened
1¼	cups white granulated sugar
3	eggs
2¾	cups all-purpose flour
1	teaspoon baking powder
1	teaspoon baking soda
1	cup evaporated milk
3	tablespoons lemon juice
1	cup chopped walnuts or almonds
2	tablespoons fresh grated lemon peel
	Lemon Glaze (see page 210)
	chopped nuts and grated lemon peel for garnish

Preheat oven to 325°F, and lightly grease a 10-inch tube pan.

In a large bowl, cream the butter and gradually add the sugar, until light and fluffy.

Beat in the eggs, one at a time.

In a medium bowl, combine the flour, baking powder and baking soda.

In a small bowl, combine the milk and lemon juice.

Alternately, beat the flour and milk mixtures into the butter mixture; beat until smooth.

Stir in the nuts and lemon peel.

Spoon into the prepared tube pan.

Bake at 325°F for 50–60 minutes, or until a toothpick inserted in the center comes out clean.

Cool, in the pan, for 20 minutes on a wire rack.

Remove from the pan and cool completely.

Drizzle with the Lemon Glaze, and sprinkle with nuts and peel garnish.

Makes one 10-inch tube cake

Chocolate Cherry Cake

★ ★ ★ ★ ★ ★ ★ ★ ★ ★ ★ ★ ★

1½   cups all-purpose flour
¾   cup white granulated sugar
¼   cup cocoa powder
1   teaspoon baking soda
⅛   teaspoon salt
1   10 ounce jar maraschino cherries, drained and
     chopped (reserve the liquid)
⅓   cup vegetable oil
¼   cup water
1   tablespoon cider vinegar
1   teaspoon vanilla extract

Preheat oven to 350°F, and lightly grease and flour a 9x9-inch baking pan.

In a large bowl, toss together the flour, sugar, cocoa, baking soda and salt until well mixed.

Add the cherries, reserved liquid, oil, water, vinegar and vanilla; stir until thoroughly blended.

Spoon into the prepared baking pan.

Bake at 350°F for 30 minutes, or until a toothpick inserted in the center comes out clean.

Cool completely, in the pan, on a wire rack before cutting.

Makes one 9x9-inch cake

This cake is moist and delicious even without any frosting. However, if you prefer, you can spread it with a white butter cream frosting.

Chocolate Potato Cake

★ ★ ★ ★ ★ ★ ★ ★ ★ ★ ★ ★ ★

2	medium potatoes, peeled and cubed
1	cup butter
2	cups white granulated sugar
1	teaspoon vanilla extract
4	eggs, separated
2	cups all-purpose flour
½	cup cocoa powder
1	tablespoon baking powder
¾	cup milk
	Chocolate Rum Glaze (see page 209)

Preheat oven to 350°F, and lightly grease and flour a 10-inch tube pan.

Cook the potatoes (covered in boiling salted water) for 15 minutes, or until tender.

Drain, mash, and cool the potatoes. Measure 1 cup, set it aside, and save the rest for another purpose.

In a large bowl, beat the butter, sugar and vanilla until well blended.

Add the egg yolks, one at a time, beating well after each.

Add the 1 cup of potatoes and mix well.

In a large bowl, combine the flour, cocoa and baking powder.

Alternately, beat the flour mixture and the milk into the potato mixture; beat until just combined.

In a large bowl, beat the egg whites into stiff peaks.

Fold into the chocolate batter, and spoon the mixture into the prepared tube pan.

Bake at 350°F for 60–75 minutes, or until a toothpick inserted in the center comes out clean.

Cool, in the pan, for 20 minutes on a wire rack.

Remove from the pan and cool completely.

Drizzle with the Chocolate Rum Glaze.

Makes one 10-inch tube cake.

The potatoes actually give an exceptionally moist, fine crumbed, chocolate cake.

Carrot Spice Cake

1½ cups firmly-packed light brown sugar
¾ cup vegetable oil
4 eggs
1½ cups all-purpose flour
1 tablespoon baking powder
1 teaspoon salt
1 teaspoon cinnamon
½ teaspoon allspice
3 cups shredded carrot (about 6 medium)
1 cup uncooked rolled oats (instant or old fashioned)
½ cup dark raisins
½ cup chopped walnuts
Cream Cheese Frosting (see page 209)

Preheat oven to 325°F, and lightly grease a 12-inch bundt pan.

In a large bowl, beat together the brown sugar and oil.

Add the eggs, one at a time, beating well after each.

In a small bowl, combine the flour, baking powder, salt, cinnamon and allspice.

Stir into the egg mixture.

Fold in the carrots, oats, raisins and nuts; mix well.

Spoon into the prepared bundt pan.

Bake at 325°F for 55–60 minutes, or until a toothpick inserted in the center comes out clean.

Cool, in the pan, for 10 minutes on a wire rack.

Remove from the pan and cool completely.

Frost with the Cream Cheese Frosting.

Makes one 12-inch bundt cake

Easy Magic Cake

2   cups all-purpose flour
1   cup white granulated sugar
1½ teaspoons baking soda
1   16 ounce can fruit pie filling (peach, cherry, apple, or berry)
2   eggs, slightly beaten
⅔   cup vegetable oil
1   teaspoon vanilla extract (use almond extract with cherry
    pie filling)

Preheat oven to 350°F, and lightly grease and flour a 9x13-inch baking pan.

In a large bowl, combine the flour, sugar and baking soda.

In medium bowl, place the pie filling, eggs, vegetable oil and extract; stir lightly until just blended.

Make a well in the center of the dry ingredients and add the pie filling mixture all at once.

Stir just until blended; large lumps are okay.

Spoon into the prepared baking pan.

Bake at 350°F for 40–50 minutes, or until a toothpick inserted in the center comes out clean.

Cool completely, in the pan, on a wire rack.

Poke holes 1-inch into the cake, and about 3-inches apart, using the handle of a wooden spoon.

Spread the topping evenly over the cake and into the holes.

Topping:
½   cup sour cream
1   cup white granulated sugar
½   teaspoon baking soda
1   tablespoon water

In a medium sauce pan, combine all the ingredients.

Cook, stirring constantly, over medium-high heat until foamy.

Cool slightly and spread evenly over the cooled cake.

Makes one 9x13-inch cake

Hot Milk Cake

★ ★ ★ ★ ★ ★ ★ ★ ★ ★ ★ ★ ★

4	eggs
2	cups white granulated sugar
2	cups all-purpose flour
2	teaspoons baking powder
½	teaspoon salt
½	cup butter or margarine
1	cup milk
1	teaspoon vanilla extract

Preheat oven to 375°F, and lightly grease and flour a 9x13-inch baking pan.

In a large bowl, cream the eggs and sugar together until lemon-colored; set aside.

In a small bowl, combine the flour, baking powder and salt; set aside.

In a small sauce pan, melt the butter over medium-high heat.

Add the milk and bring to a boil, stirring constantly; remove from the heat.

Alternately, add the flour mixture and the milk mixture to the creamed eggs and sugar.

Stir in the vanilla and mix until just blended.

Spoon into the prepared baking pan.

Bake at 375°F for 50 minutes, or until a toothpick inserted in the center comes out clean.

Cool completely, in the pan, on a wire rack.

Serve with one of your favorite dark chocolate frosting recipes.

Makes one 9x13-inch cake

This standard white cake is almost always ready to make at a moment's notice— most of the ingredients are probably in your pantry already.

Wayne's Sweet Tater Supreme

★ ★ ★ ★ ★ ★ ★ ★ ★ ★ ★ ★ ★

1½ cups vegetable oil
2 cups white granulated sugar
4 eggs, separated
4 tablespoons hot water
2 cups sifted all-purpose flour
¼ teaspoon salt
3 teaspoons baking powder
1 teaspoon cinnamon
1 teaspoon nutmeg
1½ cups grated raw sweet potato
1 cup chopped walnuts
1 teaspoon vanilla extract
   Creamy Coconut Butter Frosting (see page 208)
   OR Cream Cheese Frosting (see page 209)

Preheat oven to 350°F, and lightly grease and flour a 9x13-inch baking pan.

In a large bowl, beat the oil and sugar together until well blended.

Add the egg yolks and gradually beat in the hot water until mixture is lemon colored.

In a medium-size bowl, sift the flour, salt, baking powder, cinnamon, and nutmeg together.

Combine the dry ingredients with the liquid all at once; beat well.

Stir in the sweet potatoes, walnuts and vanilla; mix well.

In a large, clean and dry bowl, beat the egg whites until stiff.

Fold them into the sweet potato mixture.

Spoon into the prepared baking pan.

Bake at 350°F for 30 minutes, or until a toothpick inserted in the center comes out clean.

Cool, in the pan, on a wire rack before frosting.

Frost with the Creamy Coconut Butter Frosting OR Cream Cheese Frosting.

Makes one 9x13-inch cake

Unbaked Lemon Cheesecake

★ ★ ★ ★ ★ ★ ★ ★ ★ ★ ★ ★ ★

1	Graham-Nut Crumb Crust (see page 178)
1	teaspoon clear gelatin
½	cup fresh lemon juice
8	ounces cream cheese, softened
8	ounces sweetened condensed milk
½	cup heavy cream

Prepare Graham-Nut Crumb Crust in a 9-inch spring form pan.

Chill for 30 minutes, or until firm.

In a large bowl, dissolve the gelatin in the lemon juice.

Add the softened cream cheese, condensed milk and heavy cream.

Beat with an electric mixer on high until smooth.

Spoon mixture into the prepared crust.

Cover and refrigerate overnight.

Promptly refrigerate your leftovers.

Makes one 8-inch pie

This simple dessert recipe, which can be made up a day in advance, is great plain or served with a drizzle of hot fudge sauce or a tart berry pie filling.

Peanut Butter Cookies

½	cup vegetable shortening
1	cup extra-crunchy peanut butter
½	cup white granulated sugar
½	cup firmly-packed light brown sugar
1	egg
1	cup all-purpose flour
1	teaspoon salt

In a large bowl, cream the shortening and peanut butter together.

Gradually add the sugars, creaming until light and fluffy.

Add the egg and blend well.

In a small bowl, combine the flour and salt.

Add to the peanut butter mixture; blend well.

Pour the batter onto a large sheet of waxed paper.

Form into a long "sausage" 3–4-inches in diameter.

Roll the waxed paper around the "sausage."

Refrigerate for at least 1 hour.

When ready to bake; preheat oven to 400°F.

Remove the dough from the refrigerator and discard waxed paper.

Slice sausage into thin disks ¼-inch thick.

Arrange disks on an ungreased cookie sheet, about 1-inch apart; press lightly with the back of a floured fork.

Bake at 400°F for 8–10 minutes, or until the cookies spread a bit and are lightly browned on the bottom.

Cool cookies on a wire rack.

Store in an airtight container.

Makes about 3 dozen cookies

This dough freezes great! After you wrap it in waxed paper, wrap it again with aluminum foil. It'll keep in the freezer like this for months. And you'll agree it's much tastier and less expensive than store bought brands.

Pumpkin-Chocolate Chip Cookies

★ ★ ★ ★ ★ ★ ★ ★ ★ ★ ★ ★ ★

½ cup butter or margarine, softened
1½ cups white granulated sugar
1 cup solid-pack pumpkin
1 egg, slightly beaten
1 teaspoon vanilla extract
2½ cups all-purpose flour
1 teaspoon baking soda
1 teaspoon baking powder
1 teaspoon cinnamon
1 teaspoon nutmeg
½ teaspoon salt
1 6 ounce package (1 cup) semisweet chocolate chips

Preheat oven to 350°F, and lightly butter a cookie sheet.

In a large bowl, cream the butter with the sugar until light and fluffy.

Blend in the pumpkin, egg and vanilla.

In a medium bowl, sift the flour, baking soda, baking powder, cinnamon, nutmeg and salt together.

Add to the butter mixture, blending well.

Stir in the chocolate chips.

Drop by heaping teaspoonfuls onto the prepared cookie sheet, about 2½-inches apart.

Bake at 350°F for 10–15 minutes, or until they spread a bit and are lightly browned on the bottom.

Cool cookies on a wire rack.

Store in an airtight container.

Makes about 6 dozen cookies

These cookies are Halloween favorites. I've seen grown men, as well as the children, eat them by the fistful.

Toasted Oatmeal Coconut Crisps

3	cups uncooked rolled oats (not instant)
1	cup butter or margarine, softened
1	cup firmly-packed light brown sugar
1	cup white granulated sugar
2	eggs
1½	cups all-purpose flour
½	teaspoon nutmeg
½	teaspoon salt
½	teaspoon baking soda
1	cup unsweetened shredded coconut
½	cup chopped pecans (optional)

Preheat oven to 350°F. Spread the oatmeal evenly over 2 ungreased cookie sheets and toast in the preheated oven for about 10 minutes, tossing and stirring occasionally.

In a large bowl, combine the butter, brown sugar and ½ cup of the white sugar; beat until well blended and creamy.

Add the eggs and beat until light and fluffy.

In a medium bowl, combine the flour, nutmeg, salt and baking soda.

Add the dry ingredients to the butter mixture; beat until completely mixed.

Add the toasted oatmeal, coconut and pecans.

Mix until well combined.

Although you can form cookies at this point, the dough will be easier to handle if you first cover and chill it for about 1 hour.

Using your hands, form small balls of dough about the size of a walnut.

Place the remaining ½ cup sugar in a large shallow dish.

Roll the balls in the sugar to coat completely.

Place, on lightly greased cookie sheets, about 2½-inches apart.

Using your moistened fingertips, or the bottom of a wet drinking glass, flatten each cookie into a disk about ¼-inch thick and 2-inches across.

Bake at 350°F for 8–10 minutes, or until they spread a bit and are a lightly browned on the bottom.

Cool cookies on a wire rack. Store in an airtight container.

Makes about 6 dozen cookies

Shirley's Cowboy Chocolate Chip Cookies

2	cups all-purpose flour
½	teaspoon baking powder
1	teaspoon baking soda
½	teaspoon salt
1	cup vegetable shortening
1	cup firmly-packed light brown sugar
1	cup white granulated sugar
2	eggs
2	cups uncooked instant rolled oats
1	teaspoon vanilla extract
1	12 ounce package (2 cups) semisweet chocolate chips

Preheat oven to 350°F, and lightly grease a cookie sheet.

In a large bowl, sift the flour, baking powder, baking soda and salt together; set aside.

In a large bowl, cream the shortening until light and fluffy.

Thoroughly blend in the sugars.

Add the eggs and beat until light and fluffy.

Add the flour mixture, and blend well.

At this point the dough is quite thick and difficult to manage; use a little "elbow grease" and a sturdy wooden spoon.

Stir in the rolled oats, vanilla and chocolate chips; blend thoroughly.

Drop by heaping teaspoonfuls onto the prepared cookie sheet, about 2-inches apart.

Bake at 350°F for 12–15 minutes, or until they spread a bit and are lightly browned on the bottom.

Cool cookies on a wire rack.

Store in an airtight container.

Makes about 6 dozen cookies

Shirley doesn't know a thing about cowboys— but she sure knows her chocolate chip cookies! Her family has been enjoying these delectable morsels for decades.

Reva's
Molasses Sugar Cookies

★ ★ ★ ★ ★ ★ ★ ★ ★ ★ ★ ★ ★

1½ cups white granulated sugar
¾ cup vegetable shortening, melted
2 cups all-purpose flour
¼ cup molasses
1 egg, slightly beaten
2 teaspoons baking soda
½ teaspoon ground cloves
½ teaspoon ginger
1 teaspoon cinnamon
½ teaspoon salt

Preheat oven to 375°F, and lightly grease a cookie sheet.

In a large bowl, combine 1 cup of the sugar with all the remaining ingredients.

Mix until well combined.

Although you can form cookies at this point, the dough will be easier to handle if you first cover and chill it for about 30 minutes.

Using your hands, form small balls of dough about the size of a walnut.

Place the remaining ½ cup sugar in a large shallow dish.

Roll the balls in the sugar to coat completely.

Place on the prepared cookie sheet, about 2½-inches apart.

Bake at 375°F for 10–12 minutes, or until they spread and are lightly browned on the bottom.

Cool cookies on a wire rack.

Store in an airtight container.

Makes about 6 dozen cookies

The perfect cookie to enjoy with a good cup of coffee and close neighbors.

Chocolate Nut Toffee Bars

1	cup butter or margarine, softened
1	cup confectioners' sugar
1¼	cups all-purpose flour
⅓	cup cocoa powder
1	14 ounce can sweetened condensed milk (not evaporated milk)
2	teaspoons vanilla extract
1	6 ounce package (1 cup) semisweet chocolate chips
½	cup chopped walnuts or pecans

Preheat oven to 350°F, and lightly grease a 9x13-inch baking pan.

Reserve 2 tablespoons of the butter.

In a large bowl, beat the remaining butter and sugar together until light and fluffy.

Add the flour and cocoa; mix well.

With floured hands, press into the prepared baking pan.

Bake at 350°F for 15 minutes.

Meanwhile, in a medium sauce pan, combine the reserved 2 tablespoons of butter with the condensed milk over medium heat.

Cook, stirring constantly, until the mixture thickens slightly, about 10 minutes.

Remove from heat and stir in the vanilla.

Spoon over the prebaked crust and bake for 10–15 minutes longer or until the crust is golden brown.

Remove from the oven and immediately top with the chocolate chips.

Let the pan stand for 1 minute, and spread chips evenly over the top while still warm.

Sprinkle evenly with the chopped nuts.

Cool completely on a wire rack and cut into bars.

Store in an airtight container at room temperature.

Makes 24 to 36 cookie bars

White Chocolate Chunk and Macadamia Nut Cookies

$\frac{2}{3}$ cup butter or margarine, softened
$\frac{1}{2}$ cup white granulated sugar
$\frac{1}{2}$ cup firmly-packed light brown sugar
1 large egg, slightly beaten
1 teaspoon vanilla extract
$1\frac{1}{2}$ cups all-purpose flour
2 tablespoons milk
$\frac{3}{4}$ cup coarsely chopped macadamia nuts
1 cup white chocolate, broken into small pieces

Preheat oven to 350°F, and lightly grease a cookie sheet.

In a large bowl, beat the butter, sugars, egg and vanilla together until light and fluffy.

Slowly add the flour.

Add the milk and beat until well blended.

Stir in the macadamia nuts and white chocolate.

Drop by heaping teaspoonfuls onto the prepared cookie sheet, about 2½ inches apart.

Bake, 1 sheet at a time, at 350°F for 12–15 minutes, or until they spread a bit and the edges become slightly browned and the tops look dry.

Cool, in the pan, on a wire rack for 2 minutes.

Remove from the pan, and cool cookies completely on a wire rack.

Store in an airtight container.

Makes about 2 dozen cookies

The macadamia nuts and white chocolate combine in this recipe to make a delicious treat with an uptown flavor.

Captain John's Bread Pudding with Lemon Sauce

1 quart milk
6 eggs, slightly beaten
1½ cups white granulated sugar
2 tablespoons vanilla extract
6 cups cubed stale white bread*
½ cup dark raisins
1 teaspoon cinnamon
Captain John's Sweet Lemon Sauce (see page 208)

Preheat oven to 350°F, and lightly butter a 9x13-inch baking pan.

In a large sauce pan, scald the milk over medium-high heat.

In a large bowl, combine the eggs, sugar and vanilla; mix very well.

Add the cubed bread, raisins and milk; mix well.

Pour into the prepared baking pan and sprinkle with the cinnamon.

Bake at 350°F for 40 minutes, or until a knife inserted in the center comes out clean.

Serve warm with Captain John's Sweet Lemon Sauce.

* To make the bread stale, leave the slices out on the counter-top overnight, uncovered.

Makes one 9x13-inch pan of pudding

Thanks to Captain John, now we can all enjoy this firehouse classic A truly sweet, wholesome dessert that, with a little forethought, is one of the fastest ways to satisfy many sweet-tooths all at once.

The Streit Family Southern Fruit Cobbler

★ ★ ★ ★ ★ ★ ★ ★ ★ ★ ★ ★ ★

½ cup butter or margarine
1 cup all-purpose flour
1 cup white granulated sugar
1 teaspoon baking powder
1 cup milk
2 tablespoons firmly-packed light brown sugar
2 cups fruit pie filling (peach, cherry, apple, or berry)

Preheat oven to 350°F, and place the butter in an 8x8-inch baking pan.

Place the pan in the oven to melt the butter.

Meanwhile, in a medium bowl, combine the flour, sugar, baking powder and milk; blend well with a wire whisk.

Pour batter over the melted butter. Do not stir!

In a small saucepan, over medium heat, place the fruit filling, stirring constantly just until hot.

Spoon the hot fruit evenly over the batter. Do not stir!

Bake at 350°F for 40–50 minutes.

During the last 10 minutes of baking, sprinkle the top with the brown sugar.

Cool on a wire rack.

Serve warm.

Makes one 8x8-inch fruit cobbler

This tasty fruit cobbler is easy to make — and not so hard on you at clean up time either!

Four Layer Dessert

★ ★ ★ ★ ★ ★ ★ ★ ★ ★ ★ ★ ★

½   cup butter or margarine
2   tablespoons white granulated sugar
1   cup all-purpose flour
½   cup chopped pecans
8   ounces cream cheese, softened
1   cup confectioners' sugar
3   cups refrigerated whipped topping
2   packages instant chocolate pudding mix
3   cups milk
1   tablespoon white granulated sugar
1   teaspoon vanilla extract

Preheat oven to 350°F, and lightly butter a 9x13-inch baking pan.

In a large bowl, beat the butter and 2 tablespoons of the white sugar together until light and fluffy.

Add the flour and beat well; stir in the pecans.

With buttered fingertips, press evenly into the prepared baking pan.

Bake at 350°F for 15 minutes, or until the center springs back from the touch.

Cool completely on a wire rack.

In a large bowl, beat the cream cheese and confectioners' sugar together until light and fluffy.

Completely stir in 1 cup of the refrigerated whipped topping.

Spread mixture evenly over the cooled cake.

Refrigerate at least one hour.

In a large bowl, beat the pudding mix, milk, remaining sugar and vanilla together; mix until well combined and quite thick.

Spread evenly over the cream cheese mixture.

Top with the remaining whipped topping.

Refrigerate at least 1 hour.

Garnish the top with a sprinkle of chopped pecans before slicing.

Makes one 9x13-inch cake-like dessert

A delicious dessert to serve if you really want your guests to linger over coffee. It's one of the easiest to put together, but you will have a few items in the sink at cleanup time.

Chocolate-Dipped Fruit

¼ cup semisweet chocolate chips
1 teaspoon vegetable shortening
   cherries
   strawberries
   tangerine sections

In a small double-boiler, melt the chocolate chips and shortening over medium heat.

Stir until smooth and melted.

Dip fruit halfway up in the chocolate.

Arrange on waxed paper.

Refrigerate 20 minutes or until set.

Makes about 1 dozen fruit pieces

These little beauties can dress up any fruit, cheese, or dessert platter quickly and elegantly.

Baked Raisin-Stuffed Apples

8	large Granny Smiths baking apples, cored
1	cup dark raisins
1	tablespoon butter or margarine
¾	cup firmly-packed light brown sugar
½	cup water
½	teaspoon cinnamon
¼	teaspoon nutmeg

Preheat oven to 350°F, and lightly butter a 9x13-inch baking pan.

Arrange the cored apples in the baking pan and fill the individual cavities with raisins.

In a medium frying pan, melt the butter over medium-high heat.

Add the brown sugar, water, cinnamon and nutmeg.

Cook, stirring constantly, until the mixture bubbles.

Pour the mixture evenly over the apples.

Bake, uncovered, at 350°F for 45 minutes, basting occasionally with the pan liquid.

Cool slightly on a wire rack.

Serve warm with a drizzle of the pan liquid.

Serves 8 people

This dish is wonderful to put into the oven as you sit down to eat. Serve it piping hot when you're ready for a sweet/tart dessert. Try it with a scoop of vanilla ice cream on the side and a sprinkle of chopped walnuts or pecans.

Creamy Coconut Butter Frosting

½ cup butter or margarine
1 8 ounce can evaporated skim milk
1 cup white granulated sugar
3 tablespoons all-purpose flour
2 egg yolks
1 teaspoon vanilla extract
1 cup shredded sweetened baking coconut

In a medium sauce pan, melt the butter over medium heat.

Mix in the evaporated milk, sugar, flour, egg yolks and vanilla.

Cook, stirring constantly, over medium heat for 10 minutes or until the mixture becomes quite thick.

Remove from the heat, and add the coconut. Continue stirring until the mixture cools and thickens.

Makes about 2 cups

Sweet Lemon Sauce

½ cup white granulated sugar
2 tablespoons corn starch
¼ teaspoon salt
2 cups water
¼ cup butter or margarine, melted
4 tablespoons fresh lemon juice

In a medium sauce pan, combine the sugar, cornstarch and salt; mix well.

Place over medium heat and gradually stir in the water.

Cook, stirring constantly, until the mixture boils.

Continue to cook and stir for 1 minute.

Remove from the heat and stir in the butter and lemon juice.

Serve over the bread pudding.

Makes about 2 cups

Orange Whipped Topping

½   cup heavy cream
1   tablespoon confectioners' sugar
1   tablespoon orange flavored liqueur

In a small bowl, beat the cream, sugar, and liqueur, on high speed until stiff.

Makes about 2 cups

Chocolate Rum Glaze

2   cups confectioners' sugar
¼   teaspoon rum extract
4   tablespoons milk
2   tablespoons cocoa powder

In a small bowl, combine all the ingredients until smooth and of drizzle consistency.

Makes about 1 cup

Cream Cheese Frosting

8   ounces cream cheese, softened
5   tablespoons sweet butter, softened
3   cups confectioners' sugar
1   teaspoon vanilla extract
¼   teaspoon ginger

In a small bowl, whip the cream cheese and butter together.

Slowly add the sugar and whip until mixture is smooth and free of lumps.

Stir in the vanilla and ginger.

Makes about 2 cups

Chocolate Topping

6   tablespoons butter or margarine
1   6 ounce package (1 cup) semisweet chocolate chips

In a small sauce pan, melt the butter and chocolate chips over very low heat.

Remove from heat; stir until smooth.

Makes about 1 cup

Lemon Glaze

1 cup confectioners' sugar
4–5 teaspoons fresh lemon juice

In a small bowl, combine ingredients until smooth and creamy.

Makes about ¾ cup

Rich Chocolate Sauce

8 1 ounce squares semisweet chocolate
½ cup heavy cream
2 tablespoons dark rum
   OR orange flavored liqueur

In a small double-boiler, melt the chocolate over medium heat.

Stir until smooth and melted.

Slowly whisk in the heavy cream, a little at a time, blending until smooth and thick.

Stir in the dark rum, or orange-flavored liqueur.

Serve warm.

Makes about 1 cup.

Cola Glaze

½ cup butter
6 tablespoons cola
3 tablespoons cocoa powder
1 16 ounce package (3½ cups) confectioners' sugar

In a medium saucepan, combine butter, cola and cocoa over medium heat.

Cook, stirring constantly, until the mixture boils.

Pour over the confectioners' sugar and stir until smooth and creamy.

Spread over hot cake and cool before cutting.

Makes about 1 cup

BLISSFUL BEVERAGES

 **BEVERAGES**

★ ★ ★ ★ ★ ★ ★ ★ ★ ★ ★ ★ ★ ★

★ ★ ★ ★ ★ ★ ★ ★ ★ ★ ★ ★ ★ ★

Blissful Beverages

Here's an assortment of refreshing beverages. They are all tasty and quite nutritious. I've varied the ingredient amounts so that you can choose just the right beverage, for just the right occasion, and as always, you can increase or decrease the amount of ingredients to suit your own purposes.

Don't underestimate the amount of liquid your guests will drink, especially on a hot day. Beverages with a lot of fruit juice are a wonderful way to replenish lost nutrients, before, during and after a hard days work.

While all the beverages are nonalcoholic, you might want to try a jigger of spiced rum or vodka in some of them. Of course, I recommend this only when you're off duty.

Cantaloupe Cooler

2 cups cantaloupe chunks
½ cup unsweetened pineapple juice
1 teaspoon lime juice

Combine all the ingredients in blender container.

Blend 1 minute or until smooth.

Pour into a tall cocktail glass packed with ice.

Garnish with a fruit kabob.

Serve immediately.

Serves 2 people

Note: When cantaloupe is in season, cut ripe, peeled melon sections into chunks or make melon balls. Place the fruit in freezer containers and add regular or diet ginger ale to cover and freeze. Serve the melon in the middle of winter, in this shake, or as a dessert. Do not thaw completely; the fruit should still have tiny ice crystals in it for optimum flavor and texture.

An excellent source of Vitamin A, Vitamin C and fiber.

Strawberry Freeze

2   cups sliced strawberries
1   cup prepared lemonade
8   ice cubes

Combine the strawberries and lemonade in blender container.

Blend 1 minute.

Gradually add the ice and blend until smooth.

Pour into a tall cocktail glass.

Garnish with a strawberry slice.

Serve immediately.

Serves 2 people

Pineapple Cooler

1   46 ounce container unsweetened pineapple juice
2   tablespoons lemon juice
1   6 ounce container frozen orange juice concentrate
1   10 ounce bottle club soda

Mix the juices and orange juice concentrate in a large plastic container.

Refrigerate.

Just before serving, add the chilled club soda.

Pour into a tall cocktail glass packed with ice.

Garnish with half an orange slice.

Serve immediately.

Serves 8 people

Fuzzy Wuzzy

1	cup fresh orange juice
1	6 ounce can apricot nectar
½	cup ginger ale

In a tall cocktail glass, packed with ice, combine the juices.

Top with the ginger ale.

Garnish with half an orange slice.

Serve immediately.

Serves 2 people

Frozen Fruit Frostie

1	ripe banana
5	large strawberries
½	cup fresh orange juice
6	cups ice cubes

Combine the banana, strawberries, and orange juice in blender container.

Blend 1 minute.

Gradually add the ice and blend until smooth.

Pour into a tall cocktail glass.

Garnish with a strawberry.

Serve immediately.

Serves 2 people

Dairy Delights

Peach Dream:

1   fresh ripe peach
1   8 ounce container light peach nonfat yogurt
¼   teaspoon almond extract
4–6 ice cubes

Peel the peach and cut into chunks.

Combine the peach, yogurt, and almond extract in blender container.

Blend 2 minutes.

Gradually add the ice and blend until smooth.

Pour into a tall cocktail glass.

Garnish with a peach wedge.

Serve immediately.

Serves 2 people

Variations

Strawberry Dream: Substitute ¾ cup strawberries (fresh or frozen, unsweetened) and one 8 ounce container light strawberry nonfat yogurt for the peach and peach yogurt in the above recipe. Omit the almond extract. Proceed as above.

Banana Dream: Substitute 1 small banana and one 8 ounce container light vanilla nonfat yogurt for the peach and peach yogurt. Omit the almond extract. Proceed as above. Top with cinnamon.

Blueberry Dream: Substitute ½ cup blueberries and one 8 ounce container light lemon flavored yogurt for the peach and peach yogurt. Omit the almond extract. Proceed as above.

Delicious flavor and an extra bonus of calcium

Orange Smoothie

1	6 ounce container frozen orange juice concentrate
1	cup low-fat (2%) milk
$\frac{1}{4}$	cup water
$\frac{1}{2}$	teaspoon vanilla extract
8–10	ice cubes

Combine the orange juice concentrate, milk, water and vanilla in blender container.

Blend 2 minutes.

Gradually add the ice and blend until smooth, (crushing the ice before adding it to the blender speeds up this process).

Pour into a tall cocktail glass.

Garnish with an orange slice.

Serve immediately.

Serves 4 people

Variations

Pineapple Smoothie: Substitute one 6 ounce container unsweetened pineapple juice concentrate for the orange juice concentrate. Proceed as above.

Tropical Smoothie: Substitute 1 medium papaya or mango (be sure it is very ripe) for the orange juice concentrate. Omit the vanilla and add 2 tablespoons of sugar. Proceed as above.

Apple Pie Smoothie

1	cup unsweetened apple juice
1	8 ounce container plain nonfat yogurt
2	tablespoons honey
$\frac{1}{8}$	teaspoon apple pie spice
4–6	ice cubes

Combine the apple juice, yogurt, honey and apple pie spice in blender container.

Blend 1 minute.

Gradually add the ice and blend until smooth.

Pour into a tall cocktail glass.

Garnish with an apple wedge.

Serve immediately.

Serves 2 people

Iced Cappuccino

2	cups low-fat (2%) milk
4	teaspoons decaffeinated instant coffee
1	tablespoon sugar
$\frac{1}{2}$	teaspoon vanilla extract
$\frac{1}{4}$	teaspoon ground cinnamon
4–6	ice cubes

Combine the milk, coffee powder, sugar, vanilla and cinnamon in blender container.

Blend 1 minute.

Gradually add the ice and blend until smooth.

Pour into a tall cocktail glass.

Garnish with a sprinkle of nutmeg.

Serve immediately.

Serves 2 people

Low Calorie Fruit Coolers

$\frac{1}{3}$ cup apple juice
$\frac{2}{3}$ cup plain (unsweetened) seltzer
twist of orange, lemon or lime peel

In a tall cocktail glass, packed with ice, combine the juice and seltzer.

Stir well.

Garnish with a twist of peel.

Serve immediately.

Serves 1 person

Variations

Substitute white grape juice, cranberry juice cocktail, pineapple juice, or grapefruit juice for the apple juice. Proceed as above.

Substitute low calorie ginger ale or low calorie citrus flavored soda for the seltzer. Proceed as above.

These coolers have a fresh, inviting taste and are very light on calories.

Iced Teaser

¹⁄₃ **cup cranberry juice cocktail**
²⁄₃ **cup lemon flavored herb tea**

In a tall cocktail glass, packed with ice, combine the juice and tea.

Stir well.

Garnish with a lemon wedge.

Serve immediately.

Serves 1 person

Variations

¹⁄₃ **cup apple juice**
²⁄₃ **cup orange spice flavored herbal tea**

Proceed as above.

Garnish with a half an orange slice.

¹⁄₃ **cup apple juice**
²⁄₃ **cup cranberry or raspberry flavored herbal tea**

Proceed as above.

Garnish with a lemon wedge.

Make up a big batch on a hot July afternoon, and you'll guarantee your popularity.

Lemon Delight

★ ★ ★ ★ ★ ★ ★ ★ ★ ★ ★ ★ ★ ★

$\frac{1}{3}$ cup white grape juice
$\frac{1}{3}$ cup lemon flavored herbal tea
$\frac{1}{3}$ cup low calorie lemon lime soda

In a tall cocktail glass, packed with ice, combine the juice and tea.

Top with the soda.

Garnish with mint sprigs, a thin slice of orange or lemon, or a fruit kabob.

Serve immediately.

Serves 1 person

Variation

Substitute unsweetened fruit flavored seltzer for the lemon lime soda.

Sun Tea

★ ★ ★ ★ ★ ★ ★ ★ ★ ★ ★ ★ ★ ★

$1\frac{1}{2}$ quarts cool water
8   herbal tea bags
1   lemon, cut into wedge
     sugar or artificial sweetener (optional)

Fill a clean $1\frac{1}{2}$ quart glass jug with the water.

Add the tea bags.

Put the lid on the jug and let stand in the sun or on the kitchen counter until the tea reaches desired strength (15–30 minutes).

Remove the tea bags and sweeten if desired with sugar or artificial sweetener.

Pour into a tall cocktail glass packed with ice.

Garnish with a wedge of lemon.

Serve immediately.

Store any remaining tea in the refrigerator.

Serves 4–6 people

Index

I hope you've enjoyed this book, and please remember to change the batteries
in your smoke detector twice a year.